THE KOREAN VERBS GUIDE
Vol. 1

written and designed by
Talk To Me In Korean

The **Korean Verbs** Guide Vol.1
한국어 학습자가 반드시 알아야 할 **동사 가이드**

1판 1쇄 · 1st edition published	2013. 12. 2.
개정판 1쇄 · 1st revised edition published	2025. 4. 7.

지은이 · Written by	Talk To Me In Korean
책임편집 · Edited by	안효진 Hyojin Ahn, 스테파니 베이츠 Stephanie Bates
디자인 · Designed by	선윤아 Yoona Sun
일러스트 · Illustrations by	장성원 Sungwon Jang
사진 · Photographs by	라이언 카발 Ryan Cabal
녹음 · Voice Recordings by	안효진 Hyojin Ahn
펴낸곳 · Published by	롱테일북스 Longtail Books
펴낸이 · Publisher	이수영 Suyoung Lee
편집 · Copy-edited by	김보경 Florence Kim
주소 · Address	04033 서울특별시 마포구 양화로 113, 3층(서교동, 순흥빌딩)
	3rd Floor, 113 Yanghwa-ro, Mapo-gu, Seoul, KOREA
이메일 · E-mail	editor@ltinc.net
ISBN	978-1-942791-60-7 13710

TTMIK - TALK TO ME IN KOREAN

THE KOREAN VERBS GUIDE

Vol.1

한국어 학습자가 반드시 알아야 할
동사 가이드

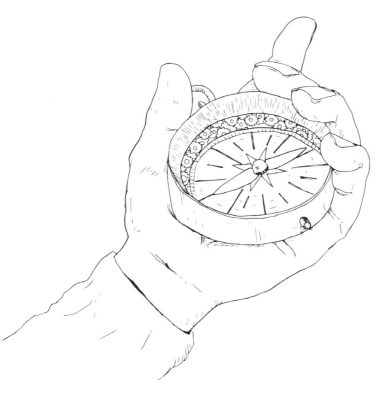

Index for Volume 1

Index for Volume 2

How To Use This Book

This book is designed to help you understand how "100 of the most commonly used Korean verbs" are conjugated and used. If you are just starting to learn Korean, going through all the verbs in the books one by one can be a good idea, but if you already know some Korean and want to enhance your grammar skills related to specific verbs, feel free to just look up those words and practice using them. In addition to the conjugation tables, you will see many sample sentences and quizzes to help you become more comfortable in using the verbs, so be sure to keep practicing and reviewing!

You can download the audio recordings for the words and sample sentences used in this book at https://talktomeinkorean.com/audio.

Using the "하다" column as a guide, you can easily translate all of the sentences in this chart. Simply switch the verb you are studying with 하다 in the example sentences. Spaces that do not have any conjugations in them mean that specific conjugation is impossible.

하다
ha-da

Present	Past	Future / Guessing	Present Progressive
해요	했어요	할 거예요	하고 있어요
I do.	I did.	I will do.	I'm doing.

Imperative *(From most to least formal)*

하세요	해요	해	해라
Please do.	*Please do.*	*Do.*	*Do.*

Modifier

한	하는	할	하던	했던
(someone) who did/has done (something) someone did	*(someone) who does/is doing (something) one does/is doing*	*(someone) who will do/is going to do (something) one will do/is going to do*	*(someone) who used to do (something) one used to do*	*(someone) who did/used to do (something) one did/used to do*

Want

할 수 있어요 → 하고 싶어요

하고 싶어요

I want to do.

Can

할 수 있어요

I can do.

Don't (Imperative)

하지 마세요

(Please) don't do.

Whether or not

하는지	했는지	할지
Whether one does/is doing or not When/Where/Who/ What/Why/How + one does/will do	*Whether one did or not When/Where/Who/ What/Why/How + one did*	*Whether one will do or not When/Where/Who/ What/Why/How + one will do*

(tell someone) that

한다고

(tell someone)/(heard) that one is doing

(tell someone) to

하라고

(tell someone) to do

General Rules of Verb Conjugation in Korean

Action verbs and Descriptive verbs

In English, words like "pretty," "big," and "important" are categorized as adjectives, whereas words like "to add," "to jump," "to study" are categorized as verbs. However, most Korean equivalents of English adjectives are originally in the infinitive form and are treated like verbs, therefore they must be conjugated to be used in the "modifier" format, which works similarly to English adjectives.

For example, "비싸다" is a descriptive verb (adjective in the infinitive form) that would translate to "to be expensive." To use it as an adjective, you need to conjugate it to the adjective form, 비싼 (present tense), 비쌀 (future tense), or 비쌌던 (past tense). In English, this kind of difference is expressed through tense change of the "be" verb, but in Korean, the conjugation of the verb itself can contain the role of the "be" verb.

Examples

크다 = to be big (descriptive verb)
큰 = big (base adjective form)

크다 = to grow (action verb)
큰 = that which has grown; grew (past tense adjective form)

Formality Levels

In Korean, there are several levels of formality. Formality levels on the more "formal" side are generally called 존댓말, and the rest are called 반말. 존대 means "to treat with respect,"

The Korean Verbs Guide - Vol.1

while 반 means "half." Although you cannot "half" speak to someone, 반말 is used with someone who you are certain is younger than you or is the same age. 존댓말 is used with everyone else. It is not appropriate to use 반말 without the other person's consent; therefore, if you are not sure which formality level to use, it is best to start off using 존댓말.

There are two main (among many) types of 존댓말 endings: -(아/어/여)요 and -(스)ㅂ니다 (e.g. 가요, 갑니다). The -(아/어/여)요 form is the more commonly used ending for 존댓말, whereas -(스)ㅂ니다 is generally used in more formal settings. If you put -아, -어, or -여 at the end of a verb stem (without -요), it becomes 반말.

If a verb's dictionary form (infinitive) is 먹다, the 반말 form is 먹어, and the 존댓말 forms are 먹어요, 먹습니다, etc.

Dictionary Form (Infinitive)

Every verb in Korean ends with -다. In most cases, before you conjugate the verb into different tenses and voices, you drop the -다 from the end of the verb and you are left with the verb stem. With the verb stem, you then conjugate the verb. When you apply a conjugation rule to a verb, be sure to remove the -다. For example, if the verb is 잡다 in the infinitive, remove the -다, and the remaining verb stem is 잡. From there, you can add various endings.

-아, -어, or -여

For many Korean verb conjugations, the verb stem is followed by -아, -어, or -여. If the sentence is in 반말, the verb will end there to make a present tense statement. If the sentence is in 존댓말, you need to add -요 at the end in addition to 아, -어, or -여. To determine which of these endings to use with a verb stem, simply look at the last syllable of the verb stem: if it ends with the vowel ㅗ or ㅏ, you add -아; if it ends with any other vowel, you add -어; and when verb stem's last syllable is 하, you add -여. When -하 and -여 are combined, it becomes 해. You will see these suffixes often in many conjugations, and these suffixes can also be followed by other sentence endings.

Present Tense = -아/어/여요

The present tense in Korean covers a wider range of tenses than in English. Therefore, a sentence in the present tense in Korean, e.g. "가요," can be translated to "I go," "I'm going," "I'm going to go," or even "I will go."

To construct a present tense sentence in Korean, add -아요, -어요, or -여요 after the verb stem. You can simply drop -요 at the end to change this to 반말.

Examples
예쁘다 = to be pretty
예뻐요 = It is pretty. (존댓말)
예뻐 = It is pretty. (반말)

일하다 = to work
일해요 = I work.; I am working.; I am going to work. (존댓말)
일해 = I work.; Get to work. (반말)

Past Tense = -았/었/였어요

Add -았어요, -었어요, or -였어요 after the verb stem to form a past tense statement. In most cases, it suffices to use -았어요, -었어요, or -였어요, but in some cases, there is an extra -었 added between -았/었/였 and -어요 to form -았었어요, -었었어요, or -였었어요. This refers to an event that happened long ago or earlier than another past event. There are many variations of the past tense, but just remember that the suffixes -았/었/였 are almost always used to end a sentence in the past tense.

Future Tense = -(으)ㄹ 거예요

-(으)ㄹ in itself has a meaning related to the future, and by saying "-(으)ㄹ 거예요," you are literally saying "It's that I will...." If the verb stem ends with a consonant at the end of the last syllable, you add -을 거예요. If the verb stem ends with a vowel, add -ㄹ 거예요. This is different from the future tense, -(으)ㄹ게요, in the sense that when you say -(으)ㄹ게요, you are expecting a response (approval or reaction) from the other person, whereas when you say -(으)ㄹ 거예요, you are simply stating what your plans are.

Although -(으)ㄹ 거예요 is a future tense sentence ending, you can also use this to express your assumption about something. Depending on the context, -(으)ㄹ 거예요 can be translated as either "it will/I will/they are going to" or "I think/I assume."

Examples
있다 = to exist, to have
시간이 있다 = to have time
시간이 있을 거예요 = There will be time.; I think they have time.

Present Progressive = -고 있어요

있어요 means "to be" whereas -고 있어요 refers to a certain state that the subject is in or an action that the subject is do-ing. By adding -고 있어요 to the verb stem, you can express the meaning of "to be doing something." Even though the present tense covers a wider range of tenses in Korean, -고 있어요

is sometimes used to emphasize the fact that you are doing something "right at this moment." If you want to use this ending in 반말, you can simply drop -요 from the end.

Examples
자다 = to sleep
자요 = She sleeps.; She is sleeping.
자고 있어요 = She is sleeping.; She is in the middle of sleeping.

Present Status = -아/어/여 있어요

-아/어/여 있어요 can be considered simliar to -고 있어요, but the usage is very different. When you use a verb stem and add -아/어/여 있어요 after, it means the subject is in a state where they are still doing that action. This can not be used with just any verb, but rather with verbs that can describe a static state related to the verb. Common examples are 서다 (to stand), 앉다 (to sit), and 눕다 (to lie down). You can conjugate these to "서 있어요" to mean "they are standing," "앉아 있어요" to mean "they are sitting," and "누워 있다" to mean "they are lying (on the bed or floor)." In addition, -아/어/여 있어요 can be used with verbs in passive voice to describe how an action has been done "to" something and how that "something" remains in a static state. An example is "깨져 있다," which is 깨지다 + -아/어/여 있다, and has the meaning of "to be in a broken state" as opposed to "to get broken."

Imperative (1) = -(으)세요

In order to tell or ask someone to do something in a polite manner in 존댓말, use -(으)세요 after the verb stem. -(으)세요 comes from -(으) + -시 + -어요, where the suffix -시 is used to make the speech more honorific. In some contexts, if you add a question mark at the end or say the same thing as a question, it can be a question asking whether or not the person "does" something.

Examples

팔다 = to sell

파세요 = Please sell it.

파세요? = Do you sell it?

Imperative (2) = -아/어/여요

If you'd still like to speak in 존댓말 without using -시, but want to be a little more casual when you tell someone to do something, you can add -아/어/여요 at the end of a verb stem. When you use this sentence ending, it is in the same form as a present tense statement or a "let's" sentence, therefore you need to figure out based on the context whether it is a state- ment or an imperative sentence.

Examples

팔다 = to sell

팔아요 = They sell. / Please sell. / Let's sell.

Imperative (3) = -아/어/여

If you are familiar with the form -아/어/여요 used in an im- perative sentence, changing this 존댓말 sentence into a 반말 sentence is very simple. When you want to speak in 반말, you can simply drop the -요 at the end of the imperative form.

Examples

팔다 = to sell

팔아요 = They sell. / Please sell it.

팔아 = They sell. / Sell it.

Imperative (4) = -아/어/여라

Use this form of imperative speech when you are talking to a younger person or a group of younger people. It is usually said in a leading or commanding manner. Since this form has the nuance of talking "down" to someone, you cannot use this to someone who is older than you, someone you met for the first time, or someone you know only through business. You will often hear this in situations where one person is lightly warning another person, or when one person is calling a group of people together to have them do something. This form rarely has a positive or affectionate feeling associated with it, so be careful when you use it!

Examples
조심하다 = to be careful
조심하세요 = Please be careful.
조심해 = Be careful!; Watch out!
조심해라 = You'd better be careful, or else...

Modifier (1) = -(으)ㄴ

Used after the verb stem of an action verb, this suffix changes a verb into a modifying adjective (in the past tense) to be used in front of a noun. This is similar to the role of the English clause "which I found" or "which I bought yesterday," which is used after a noun.

Examples
찾다 = to find
찾은 = which I/he/she/they found, which they found
어제 찾은 책 = the book I found yesterday

When you add -(으)ㄴ after a descriptive verb, it has the same effect, except that the adjective will be in the present tense instead of the past tense.

Examples
예쁘다 = to be pretty

예쁜 = which/that is pretty

예쁜 옷 = pretty clothes

Modifier (2)
= -는

Used after a verb stem, this suffix changes a verb into an modifying adjective in the present tense to be used in front of a noun. This is similar to the role of a clause in English, such as "which I like" or "that I use everyday," which is used after a noun; however, in Korean, it is only used after action verbs. For descriptive verbs, -(으)ㄴ is used to mark the present tense.

Examples

가다 = to go

가는 = that I go to

매일 가는 곳 = a place that I go to every day

Modifier (3)
= -(으)ㄹ

This suffix changes the verb to a modifying adjective in the future tense. This is similar to the role of an English clause "which will start tomorrow" or "that you will see there," but used after a noun. This can be applied in the same way to both action verbs and descriptive verbs, although it is more common to be used with action verbs.

Examples

바꾸다 = to change, to switch, to exchange

바꿀 = which I will change

바꿀 부분 = parts that I will change

Modifier (4)
= -던

This suffix has a similar role to that of -(으)ㄴ, but -던 marks the discontinuation of an action or a past habit or tendency. -던 can be used to refer to something that you used to do, or were doing until something caused you to stop doing it. Therefore, if you hear -던 as opposed to -(으)ㄴ, you can assume that the action was not finished or continued, where as -(으)ㄴ would indicate that the action was completed.

Examples
먹다 = to eat
먹은 = which you ate
먹던 = which you were eating (but didn't finish)
먹은 음식 = food that you ate
먹던 음식 = leftover food

Modifier (5)
= -았/었/였던

This suffix is almost the same as -던, but because there is one more layer of past tense (pluperfect), due to -았/었/였 it stresses that fact that something happened in the past or emphasizes the discontinuation of the action or state. In many contexts, however, when used with action verbs, -았/었/였던 is considered to be redundant since -던 is a clear enough meaning on its own.

Examples
모르다 = to not know
모르던 = which I didn't know
몰랐던 = which I didn't know

With descriptive verbs, adding -았/었/였던 is the most common way to say "which was ...," but often times, if the entire sentence is in the past tense, smaller parts do not always have to be conjugated to past tense.

Examples

비싸다 = to be expensive

비쌌던 = which was expensive

비싼 옷을 샀어요 = She bought expensive clothes. (비싼 is in the present tense form, but the whole sentence is in the past tense.)

Want = -고 싶다

By adding -고 싶다 to the end of a verb stem, you are adding the meaning "I want to." The word 싶다 cannot be used as a stand-alone verb to mean "to want," therefore it must always be used with other verbs. Since 싶다 is also a verb, you can conjugate it accordingly to change it to other tenses.

Examples

배우다 = to learn

배우고 싶다 = to want to learn

배우고 싶어요 = I want to learn.

Can = -(으)ㄹ 수 있다

수 is a noun that means "possibility," "idea," or "method (for doing something)," and 있다 means "to exist" or "to have." By saying that the 수 exists (있다), you mean that you "can (do something)." Since 수 is a noun, you need to change the verb into a modifying form: if the verb stem ends with a consonant, add -을 수 있다, and if the verb stem ends with a vowel, add -ㄹ 수 있다 to the end. To say that you cannot do something, you can change the verb 있어요 to 없다, which means "to not have" or "to not exist." You can also use the word 못 in front of the verb instead of -(으)ㄹ 수 없다.

Examples

뛰다 = to run

뛸 수 있다 = to be able to run

뛸 수 있어요 = I can run.

뛸 수 없어요 = I can't run.

못 뛰어요 = I can't run.

Don't (Imperative) = -지 마세요

-지 is a suffix which is used to make negative sentences. "-지 않아요" means "it is not," "-지 못 해요" means "I can't," and "-지 마세요" means "Don't do it." -지 마세요 generally does not work with descriptive verbs, such as 예쁘다 (to be pretty) or 빠르다 (to be fast); however, there are some descriptive verbs that do work with -지 마세요, such as 늦다 (to be late) and 아프다 (to be sick/hurt). "늦지 마세요" means "don't be late" and "아프지 마세요" means "don't get sick" or "feel better soon."

Since the ending -지 마세요 originally comes from the verb 말다, which means "to not do (something)," it can also be combined with other types of verb endings, such as -지 말고, -지 말라고, etc.

Whether or not (1) = -(으/느)ㄴ지

Although -지 is used in negative sentences, -은지, -는지, or -ㄴ지 is different from -지. These suffixes are used to mean "whether or not" and are commonly used with verbs such as 묻다 (= to ask), 모르다 (= to not know), and 알다 (= to know). With action verbs, you add -는지 after the verb stem. With descriptive verbs, if the verb stem ends with a consonant, you need to add -은지, and if the verb stem ends with a vowel, you need to add -ㄴ지. To make the meaning of "whether or not" stronger, the opposite version is also added after it as well. (e.g. 큰지 안 큰지 or 가는지 안 가는지) You can -(으/느)ㄴ지 is often used with 얼마나 to mean "to ask/not know/know how big/large/much/etc something is."

Examples

크다 = to be big

큰지 = whether it is big or not

큰지 안 큰지 = whether it is big or not

얼마나 큰지 = how big it is

얼마나 큰지 알아요? = Do you know how big it is?

큰지 안 큰지 알아요? = Do you know whether it is big or not?

Whether or not (2) = -았/었/였는지

-았/었/였는지 is almost the same as -(으/느)ㄴ지 except it's used to express the past tense. Instead of adding -(으/느)ㄴ지 after a verb stem, you add -았, -었, or -였 and then add -는지. The usages are almost identical to -(으/느)ㄴ지.

Examples

끝나다 = to be finished

끝났는지 = whether it was finished or not

끝났는지 안 끝났는지 = whether it was finished or not

언제 끝났는지 = when it was finished

언제 끝났는지 알아요? = Do you know when it was finished?

끝났는지 안 끝났는지 알아요? = Do you know whether it was finished or not?

Whether or not (3) = -(으)ㄹ지

This suffix is also used to mean "whether or not," but refers to a future action or state. You can use this structure along with verbs related to speaking, hearing, deciding, notifying, etc. You can also add interrogative words such 언제 (when), 뭐 (what), 누구 (who), 어디 (where), etc. before the verb.

Examples

가다 = to go

갈지 = whether we will go

어디에 갈지 = where we will go

언제 갈지 = when we will go

(tell someone) that = -(ㄴ/는)다고

-(ㄴ/는)다고 is used to cite someone or oneself in the present tense. It can be used when you want to tell someone what a third person or what you, yourself, said. With action verbs, if the verb stem ends with a consonant, add -는다고, and if the verb stem ends with a vowel, add -ㄴ다고. With descriptive verbs, simply add -다고.

Even when you are talking about something that someone said in the past, if that person said it in the present tense at the time, you can use -(ㄴ/는)다고.

Examples

운동하다 = to exercise

운동한다고 말하다 = to say that they exercise

운동한다고 말했어요 = They said that they were exercising.

운동한다고 말해 주세요 = Tell them that I am exercising.

(tell someone) that (past tense) = -았/었/였다고

This suffix is basically the same as -(ㄴ/는)다고, but is used for past tense. If the last vowel of the verb stem is ㅗ or ㅏ, add -았다고, and if the last vowel of the verb stem is not ㅗ or ㅏ, add -었다고. However, there is one exception with the verb 하다: add -였다고 and shorten it to 했다고. This structure is used in conjunction with verbs related to speaking and hearing.

Examples

늦다 = to be late

늦었어요 = was late

늦었다고 했어요. = They said it was late.

The Korean Verbs Guide - Vol.1

이미 늦었다고 들었어요. = I heard that it was already (too) late.

(tell someone) to = -(으)라고

-(으)라고 is used when you are citing what someone told another person to do. It is usually used with verbs related to speaking, demanding, begging, etc. For example, if you want to say, "they told me to wait," you can use the verb 기다리다 (to wait) together with -(으)라고 to form "기다리라고 했어요." Other words you can use after -(으)라고 are 시키다 (to make someone do something), 지시하다 (to command), etc. When you use -(으)라고 with verbs related to begging or asking for a favor, it is nearly always necessary to change "verb stem + -(으)라고" to "verb stem + -아/어/여 달 + -라고." For example, "도와달라고 부탁했어요" means "I asked them to help me," whereas "들어달라고 부탁했어요" means "I asked them to listen to me."

If the verb stem ends with a consonant, add -으라고, and if the verb stem ends with a vowel, add -라고.

(tell someone) that (future tense) = -(으)ㄹ 거라고

-(으)ㄹ 거라고 is used when you are citing what someone else said about something he/she will do in the future. -(으)ㄹ 거라고 is rarely used on its own and is almost always followed by verbs related to speaking, writing, or other types of actions related to delivering messages. In order to say, "to say that someone did something," you can use the verb 말하다, or 하다, and say "-(으)ㄹ 거라고 말하다" or "-(으)ㄹ 거라고 하다."

Examples
만나다 = to meet
만날 거라고 = that she will meet
만날 거라고 했어요 = She said that she would meet.

친구들을 만날 거라고 했어요.

= She said that she would meet friends.

친구들을 만날 거라고 하세요.

= Tell them that she will meet friends.

If the verb stem ends with a consonant, you add -을 거라고 and if the verb stem ends with a vowel, you add -ㄹ 거라고.

Vol. 1

가다
to go; to leave

Conjugation

Present	*Past*	*Future / Guessing*	*Present Progressive*
가요	갔어요	갈 거예요	가고 있어요
gayo	gasseoyo	gal geoyeyo	gago isseoyo

Imperative

가세요	가요	가	가라
gaseyo	gayo	ga	gara

Modifier

간	가는	갈	가던	갔던
gan	ganeun	gal	gadeon	gatteon

Want	*Can*
가고 싶어요	갈 수 있어요
gago sipeoyo	gal su isseyo

Don't (Imperative)	*Whether or not*		
가지 마세요	가는지	갔는지	갈지
gaji maseyo	ganeunji	ganneunji	galji

(tell someone) that	*(tell someone) to*
간다고	가라고
gandago	garago

Sample Sentences

Track 01

1. 내년에 한국에 갈 거예요.
   I'm going to Korea next year.

2. 거기 혼자 가지 마세요.
   Please don't go there alone.

3. 내일 현우 씨 생일 파티에 가는 사람 있어요?
   Is there anyone going to Hyunwoo's birthday party tomorrow?

4. 거기 어떻게 가는지 아세요?
   Do you know how to get there?

5. 지하철 말고 버스 타고 가고 싶어요.
   I want to take the bus, not the subway.

Quiz

1. 내일 빅뱅 콘서트에 (   ).
   I'm going to a Big Bang concert tomorrow.

2. 거기 밤에 (   ).
   Please don't go there at night.

3. 다음주에 석진 씨 결혼식에 (   ) 사람 있어요?
   Is anyone going to Seokjin's wedding next week?

Answers :
1. 갈 거예요 / 2. 가지 마세요 / 3. 가는

오다

to come

Conjugation

Present	Past	Future / Guessing	Present Progressive
와요	왔어요	올 거예요	오고 있어요
wayo	wasseoyo	ol geoyeyo	ogo isseoyo

Imperative

오세요	와요	와	와라
oseyo	wayo	wa	wara

Modifier

온	오는	올	오던	왔던
on	oneun	ol	odeon	watteon

Want

오고 싶어요
ogo sipeoyo

Can

올 수 있어요
ol su isseoyo

Don't (Imperative)

오지 마세요			
oji maseyo			

Whether or not

오는지	왔는지	올지
oneunji	wanneunji	olji

(tell someone) that

온다고
ondago

(tell someone) to

오라고
orago

Sample Sentences

1. 언제 왔어요?
   When did you come?

2. 다음에 또 오고 싶어요.
   I want to come again.

3. 그저께 효진 씨랑 같이 왔던 사람 누구예요?
   Who is that person who came with Hyojin the day before yesterday?

4. 경은 씨가 언제 올지는 아무도 몰라요.
   Nobody knows when Kyeong-eun will come.

5. 부모님이랑 같이 오세요.
   Come with your parents, please.

Quiz

1. 어저께 윤아 씨랑 같이 (　　　) 사람 이름 알아요?
   Do you know the name of the person who came with Yoona yesterday?

2. 테리스 씨가 언제 (　　　) 정말 몰라요?
   You really don't know when Terris will come?

3. 다음에는 경화 씨랑 같이 (　　　).
   Please come with Kyung-hwa next time.

Answers :
1. 왔던 / 2. 올지 / 3. 오세요 or 와요.

29

많이 드세요.

Eat a lot. (Help yourself.)

먹다
to eat; to drink

Conjugation

먹다
meok-da

Present	Past	Future / Guessing	Present Progressive
먹어요	먹었어요	먹을 거예요	먹고 있어요
meogeoyo	meogeosseoyo	meogeul geoyeyo	meokgo isseoyo

Imperative

드세요	먹어요	먹어	먹어라
deuseyo	meogeoyo	meogeo	meogeora

Modifier

먹은	먹는	먹을	먹던	먹었던
meogeun	meongneun	meogeul	meokdeon	meogeotteon

Want	Can
먹고 싶어요	먹을 수 있어요
meokko sipeoyo	meogeul su isseoyo

Don't (Imperative)	Whether or not		
먹지 마세요	먹는지	먹었는지	먹을지
meokji maseyo	meongneunji	meogeonneunji	meogeulji

(tell someone) that	(tell someone) to
먹는다고	먹으라고
meongneundago	meogeurago

Sample Sentences

1. 많이 드세요.
   Eat a lot. (Help yourself.)

2. 엄마가 이거 다 먹으라고 하셨어요.
   My mom told me to eat all of this.

3. 김밥 먹고 있어요.
   I'm eating Kimbap.

4. 저는 금요일 저녁에는 늘 치킨을 먹어요.
   I always eat chicken on Friday nights.

5. 저는 피자 한 판을 혼자 다 먹을 수 있어요.
   I can eat a whole pizza by myself.

Quiz

1. 아빠가 이거 이따가 (   ) 하셨어요.
   My dad told me to eat this later.

2. 지민 씨가 비빔밥을 (   ).
   Jimin is eating Bibimbap.

3. 현정 씨는 일요일에는 항상 파스타를 (   ).
   Hyeonjeong always eats pasta on Sundays.

Answers :
1. 먹으라고 / 2. 먹고 있어요 / 3. 먹어요

보다
to see, to look, to watch

Conjugation

Present	Past	Future / Guessing	Present Progressive
봐요	봤어요	볼 거예요	보고 있어요
bwayo	bwasseoyo	bol geoyeyo	bogo isseoyo

Imperative

보세요	봐요	봐	봐라
boseyo	bwayo	bwa	bwara

Modifier

본	보는	볼	보던	봤던
bon	boneun	bol	bodeon	bwatteon

Want	Can
보고 싶어요	볼 수 있어요
bogo sipeoyo	bol su isseoyo

Don't (Imperative)	Whether or not		
보지 마세요	보는지	봤는지	볼지
boji maseyo	boneunji	bwanneunji	bolji

(tell someone) that	(tell someone) to
본다고	보라고
bondago	borago

Sample Sentences

1. 저도 눈 보고 싶어요.
   I want to see the snow, too.

2. 몇 명이 제 사진 봤는지 알 수 있어요?
   Can I know how many people saw my photo?

3. 오늘 동물원에 가서 토끼를 봤어요.
   Today I went to the zoo and saw rabbits.

4. 무슨 드라마 볼 거예요?
   Which drama are you going to watch?

5. 제 핸드폰 보지 마세요.
   Don't look at my cell phone, please.

Quiz

1. 내년에는 바다 (   ).
   I want to see the sea next year.

2. 오늘 공원에 가서 다람쥐를 (   ).
   Today I went to the park and saw squirrels.

3. 내일 무슨 영화 (   )?
   Which movie are you going to watch tomorrow?

Answers :
1. 보고 싶어요 / 2. 봤어요 / 3. 볼 거예요?

사다
to buy

Conjugation

사다
sa-da

Present	Past	Future / Guessing	Present Progressive
사요	샀어요	살 거예요	사고 있어요
sayo	sasseoyo	sal geoyeyo	sago isseoyo

Imperative

사세요	사요	사	사라
saseyo	sayo	sa	sara

Modifier

산	사는	살	사던	샀던
san	saneun	sal	sadeon	satteon

Want / Can

Want	Can
사고 싶어요	살 수 있어요
sago sipeoyo	sal su isseoyo

Don't (Imperative) / Whether or not

Don't (Imperative)	Whether or not		
사지 마세요	사는지	샀는지	살지
saji maseyo	saneunji	sanneunji	salji

(tell someone) that / (tell someone) to

(tell someone) that	(tell someone) to
산다고	사라고
sandago	sarago

Sample Sentences

1. 제가 산 우유를 누가 벌써 다 마셨어요.
   Someone already drank the milk I bought.

2. 이거랑 똑같은 신발 어디서 살 수 있어요?
   Where can I buy shoes, exactly like these ones?

3. 경화 씨가 무슨 가방 샀는지 알아요?
   Do you know which bag Kyung-hwa bought?

4. 이거랑 똑같은 컴퓨터 효진 씨도 산다고 했어요.
   Hyojin said she was buying the same computer as this one.

5. 어떤 색깔을 살지 모르겠어요.
   I don't know which color I should buy.

Quiz

1. 제가 (   ) 케이크를 누가 벌써 다 먹었어요.
   Someone already ate the cake I bought.

2. 현우 씨가 남대문에서 무슨 카메라 (   ) 알아요?
   Do you know which camera Hyunwoo bought at Namdaemun?

3. 저거랑 똑같은 선글라스 민수 씨도 (   ) 했어요.
   Minsoo said he was buying the same sunglasses as those.

있다

to be (there),
to have, to exist

Conjugation

있다
it-da

Present	Past	Future / Guessing	Present Progressive
있어요	있었어요	있을 거예요	–
isseoyo	isseosseoyo	isseul geoyeyo	

Imperative

–	–	–	–

Modifier

–	있는	있을	있던	있었던
	inneun	isseul	itteon	isseotteon

Want	Can
있고 싶어요	–
itgo sipeoyo	

Don't (Imperative)	Whether or not		
–	있는지	있었는지	있을지
	inneunji	isseoneunji	isseulji

(tell someone) that	(tell someone) to
있다고	있으라고
ittago	isseurago

Sample Sentences

1. 분명 여기에 있었어요.
   It was definitely here.

2. 내일까지 여기 있을 거예요.
   I'm going to be here until tomorrow.

3. 지금 어디에 있어요?
   Where are you now?

4. 5분 전에 여기 있던 사람 어디 갔어요?
   Where did the person who was here five minutes ago go?

5. 선생님이 저보고 여기 있으라고 하셨어요.
   My teacher told me to be here.

Quiz

1. 다음주까지 여기 (   ).
   I'm going to be here until next week.

2. 지금 누구랑 (   )?
   Who are you with now?

3. 아까 엄마가 저보고 여기 (   ) 하셨어요.
   My mom told me to be here before.

Answers :
1. 있을 거예요 / 2. 있어요 / 3. 있으라고

The Korean Verbs Guide - Vol.1

없다

to be not (there), to not have, to not exist

Conjugation

없다
eop-da

Present	Past	Future / Guessing	Present Progressive
없어요	없었어요	없을 거예요	–
eopsseoyo	eopsseosseoyo	eopseul geoyeyo	

Imperative

–	–	–	–

Modifier

–	없는	없을	없던	없었던
	eomneun	eopsseul	eopdeon	eopsseotteon

Want	Can
–	–

Don't (Imperative)	Whether or not		
–	없는지	없었는지	없을지
	eomneunji	eopsseonneunji	eopsseulji

(tell someone) that	(tell someone) to
없다고	–
eopdago	

Sample Sentences

1. 저 아직 차 없어요.
   I don't have a car yet.

2. 돈이 없다고 하더라고요.
   He said he didn't have money.

3. 왜 저는 없는 사람 취급해요?
   Why do you treat me like I'm not here?

4. 서랍 속에는 없었어요.
   It wasn't in the drawer.

5. 있을지 없을지 저도 잘 모르겠어요.
   I'm not sure if it's going to be there or not.

Quiz

1. 저 아직 스마트폰 (   ).
   I don't have a smartphone yet.

2. 정수 씨는 시간이 (   ) 하더라고요.
   Jeongsu said she didn't have time.

3. 제 지갑 속에는 (   ).
   It wasn't in my wallet.

Answers :
1. 없어요 / 2. 없다고 / 3. 없었어요

45

잘 자요.

Sleep well. (Goodnight.)

자다
to sleep

Conjugation

Present	Past	Future / Guessing	Present Progressive
자요 jayo	잤어요 jasseoyo	잘 거예요 jal geoyeyo	자고 있어요 jago isseoyo

Imperative

주무세요 jumuseyo	자요 jayo	자 ja	자라 jara

Modifier

잔 jan	자는 janeun	잘 jal	자던 jadeon	잤던 jatteon

Want	Can
자고 싶어요 jago sipeoyo	잘 수 있어요 jal su isseoyo

Don't (Imperative)	Whether or not		
자지 마세요 jaji maseyo	자는지 janeunji	잤는지 janneunji	잘지 jalji

(tell someone) that	(tell someone) to
잔다고 jandago	자라고 jarago

Sample Sentences

1. 잘 자요.
   Sleep well. (Goodnight.)

2. 잘 잤어요?
   Have you slept well? (How did you sleep?)

3. 여기서 자지 마세요.
   Don't sleep here, please.

4. 저는 매일 11시에 자요.
   I go to sleep at 11 o'clock every day.

5. 지금 옆방에서 아기가 자고 있어요.
   A baby is sleeping in the next room now.

Quiz

1. 지금 (   ).
   Don't sleep now, please.

2. 저는 평일에는 매일 12시에 (   ).
   I go to sleep at 12 o'clock every day during the weekdays.

3. 지금 방 안에서 동생이 (   ).
   My little brother is sleeping in the room now.

하다
to do

Conjugation

하다
ha-da

Present	Past	Future / Guessing	Present Progressive
해요	했어요	할 거예요	하고 있어요
haeyo	haesseoyo	hal geoyeyo	hago isseoyo

Imperative

하세요	해요	해	해라
haseyo	haeyo	hae	haera

Modifier

한	하는	할	하던	했던
han	haneun	hal	hadeon	haetteon

Want

하고 싶어요
hago sipeoyo

Can

할 수 있어요
hal su isseoyo

Don't (Imperative)

하지 마세요
haji maseyo

Whether or not

하는지	했는지	할지
haneunji	haenneunji	halji

(tell someone) that

한다고
handago

(tell someone) to

하라고
harago

51

Sample Sentences

1. 아까 뭐 했어요?
   What did you do before?

2. 할지 안 할지 빨리 결정해 주세요.
   Please decide quickly whether you are going to do it or not.

3. 지금 조금 피곤하기는 한데 할 수 있어요.
   I'm a little tired but I can do it.

4. 언제 할 거예요?
   When are you going to do it?

5. 선생님이 빨리 하라고 하셨어요.
   The teacher said to do it quickly.

Quiz

1. 거기 안에서 뭐 (   )?
   What did you do in there?

2. 어디에서 (   )?
   Where are you going to do?

3. 엄마가 내일 (   ) 말씀하셨어요?
   My mom said to do it tomorrow.

Answers :
1. 했어요 / 2. 할 거예요 / 3. 하라고

놀다

to play, to hang out with (someone)

Conjugation

놀다
nol-da

Present	Past	Future / Guessing	Present Progressive
놀아요	놀았어요	놀 거예요	놀고 있어요
norayo	norasseoyo	nol geoyeyo	nolgo isseoyo

Imperative

노세요	놀아요	놀아	놀아라
noseyo	norayo	nora	norara

Modifier

논	노는	놀	놀던	놀았던
non	noneun	nol	noldeon	noratteon

Want		Can	
놀고 싶어요		놀 수 있어요	
nolgo sipeoyo		nol su isseoyo	

Don't (Imperative)		Whether or not		
놀지 마세요		노는지	놀았는지	놀지
nolji maseyo		noneunji	noranneunji	nolji

(tell someone) that		(tell someone) to	
논다고		놀라고	
nondago		nollago	

Sample Sentences

1. 어디서 놀지 정했어요?
   Have you decided where to play?

2. 어제 하루종일 놀았어요.
   I played all day long yesterday.

3. 어렸을 때 어떻게 놀았는지 기억나요?
   Do you remember how you used to play when you were little?

4. 엄마가 집에만 있지 말고 밖에 나가서 놀라고 하셨어요.
   My mom told me not to just stay at home, but to go out and play.

5. 운동장에서 놀던 아이들이 이제는 모두 집에 갔어요.
   All the kids who were playing in the playground went home already.

Quiz

1. 어제 자기 전에 (   ).
   Yesterday, I played before I went to bed.

2. 초등학교 다닐 때 누구랑 (   ) 기억나요?
   Do you remember who you used to play with when you were in elementary school?

3. 아빠가 집에서 컴퓨터 게임만 하지 말고 밖에 나가서 친구들하고
   (   ) 하셨어요.
   My dad told me not to only play computer games at home, but to go out and play with friends.

Answers :
1. 놀았어요 / 2. 놀았는지 / 3. 놀라고

55

멀다
to be far

Conjugation

멀다
meol-da

Present	Past	Future / Guessing	Present Progressive
멀어요	멀었어요	멀 거예요	-
meoreoyo	meoreosseoyo	meol geoyeyo	

Imperative

-	-	-	-

Modifier

먼	-	멀	멀던	멀었던
meon		meol	meoldeon	meoreotteon

Want	Can
-	멀 수 있어요
	meol su isseoyo

Don't (Imperative)	Whether or not		
-	먼지	멀었는지	멀지
	meonji	meoreonneunji	meolji

(tell someone) that	(tell someone) to
멀다고	-
meoldago	

Sample Sentences

Track
11

1. 걸어가기에는 너무 멀어요.
   It's too far to walk there.

2. 서울에서 부산까지 멀어요?
   Is it far from Seoul to Busan?

3. 굉장히 멀다고 들었어요.
   I heard it's really far.

4. 그렇게 먼 곳에는 가고 싶지 않아요.
   I don't want to go somewhere so far away.

5. 얼마나 먼지 알아요?
   Do you know how far it is?

Quiz

1. 자전거 타고 가기에는 너무 (   ).
   It's too far to bike.

2. 시에틀에서 샌프란시스코까지 (   )?
   Is it far from Seattle to San Francisco?

3. 별로 안 (   ) 들었어요.
   I heard it's not that far.

Answers :
1. 멀어요 / 2. 멀어요 / 3. 멀다고

가깝다

to be close

Conjugation

가깝다
ga-kkap-da

Present	Past	Future / Guessing	Present Progressive
가까워요	가까웠어요	가까울 거예요	–
gakkawoyo	gakkawosseoyo	gakkaul geoyeyo	

Imperative

–	–	–	–

Modifier

가까운	–	가까울	가깝던	가까웠던
gakkaun		gakkaul	gakkapdeon	gakkawotteon

Want	Can
–	가까울 수 있어요
	gakkaul su isseoyo

Don't (Imperative)	Whether or not		
–	가까운지	가까웠는지	가까울지
	gakkaunji	gakkawonneunji	gakkaulji

(tell someone) that	(tell someone) to
가깝다고	–
gakkapdago	

The Korean Verbs Guide - Vol.1

Sample Sentences

1. 회사에서 집까지 가까워요.
   My office and my house are close.

2. 가깝다고 들었는데 실제로 가 보니 좀 멀었어요.
   I heard it was close, but when I actually went there, it was a bit far.

3. 아마 가까울 거예요.
   I think it'll be close.

4. 가까운지 먼지, 지도에서 확인해 주세요.
   Please check the map to see if it's close or far away.

5. 주말에 가까운 곳으로 드라이브 가고 싶어요.
   I want to go for a drive to a nearby place on the weekend.

Quiz

1. 집에서 지하철 역까지 (   ).
   My house and the subway station are close.

2. (   ) 들었는데 정말 (   )?
   I heard it was close; is it really close?

3. (   ) 먼지, 물어봐 주세요.
   Please ask them if it's near or far.

Answers :
1. 가까워요 / 2. 가깝다고, 가까워요 / 3. 가까운지

61

전에 살던 곳에 비해
이곳이 더 조용하네요.

This place is quieter than the place I used to live in.

살다
to live

Conjugation

sal-da

Present	Past	Future / Guessing	Present Progressive
살아요	살았어요	살 거예요	살고 있어요
sarayo	sarasseoyo	sal geoyeyo	salgo isseoyo

Imperative

사세요	살아요	살아	살아라
saseyo	sarayo	sara	sarara

Modifier

산	사는	살	살던	살았던
san	saneun	sal	saldeon	saratteon

Want	Can
살고 싶어요	살 수 있어요
salgo sipeoyo	sal su isseoyo

Don't (Imperative)	Whether or not		
살지 마세요	사는지	살았는지	살지
salji maseyo	saneunji	saranneunji	salji

(tell someone) that	(tell someone) to
산다고	살라고
sandago	sallago

The Korean Verbs Guide - Vol.1

64

Sample Sentences

1. 저는 서울에 살아요.
   I live in Seoul.

2. 저는 나중에 2층 집에서 살고 싶어요.
   Later on, I want to live in a two story house.

3. 전에 살던 곳에 비해 이곳이 더 조용하네요.
   This place is quieter than the place I used to live in.

4. 지금 사는 집에서 얼마나 더 살지 아직 잘 모르겠어요.
   I'm not sure how much longer I will stay in the house that I live in now.

5. 엄마는 결혼하시기 전에 외삼촌 가족이랑 살았다고 하셨어요.
   My mom said she used to live with my uncle and his family before she got married.

Quiz

1. 저는 런던에 (   ).
   I live in London.

2. 저는 나중에 바닷가 옆에 있는 집에서 (   ).
   Later on, I want to live in a house next to the sea.

3. 2년 전에 (   ) 곳에 비해 이 곳이 더 넓어요.
   This place is bigger compared to the place I used to live in two years ago.

Answers :
1. 살아요 / 2. 살고 싶어요 or 살고 싶어요 / 3. 살았던 or 살던

65

도와주다

to help

Conjugation

도와주다
do·wa·ju·da

Present	Past	Future / Guessing	Present Progressive
도와줘요	도와줬어요	도와줄 거예요	도와주고 있어요
dowajwoyo	dowajwosseoyo	dowajul geoyeyo	dowajugo isseoyo

Imperative

도와주세요	도와줘요	도와줘	도와줘라
dowajuseyo	dowajwoyo	dowajwo	dowajwora

Modifier

도와준	도와주는	도와줄	도와주던	도와줬던
dowajun	dowajuneun	dowajul	dowajudeon	dowajeotteon

Want

도와주고 싶어요
dowajugo sipeoyo

Can

도와줄 수 있어요
dowajul su isseoyo

Don't (Imperative)

도와주지 마세요
dowajuji maseyo

Whether or not

도와주는지	도와줬는지	도와줄지
dowajuneunji	dowajwonneunji	dowajulji

(tell someone) that

도와준다고
dowajundago

(tell someone) to

도와주라고
dowajurago

Sample Sentences

1. 혼자서 하게 도와주지 마세요.
   Please don't help him so that he can do it by himself.

2. 저 내일 이사하는 데 좀 도와줄 수 있어요?
   I'm moving tomorrow, so do you think you can help me out?

3. 언니가 제 숙제를 도와주고 있어요.
   My older sister is helping me with my homework.

4. 동생 좀 도와줘라.
   Help your (younger) brother.

5. 내일 행사에서 저를 도와줄 사람들을 찾고 있어요.
   I'm looking for people who can help me at tomorrow's event.

Quiz

1. 저 다음주에 이사하는 데 좀 (   )?
   I'm moving next week, so do you think you can help me out?

2. 형이 동생 숙제를 (   ).
   My older brother is helping my younger sister with her homework.

3. 이번 일요일에 모임에서 저를 (   ) 사람들을 찾고 있어요.
   I'm looking for people who can help me at this Sunday's meet-up.

Answers :
1. 도와줄 수 있어요 / 2. 도와주고 있어요 / 3. 도와줄

쉽다
to be easy

Conjugation

Present	Past	Future / Guessing	Present Progressive
쉬워요 swiwoyo	쉬웠어요 swiwosseoyo	쉬울 거예요 swiul geoyeyo	–

Imperative			
–	–	–	–

Modifier				
쉬운 swiun	–	쉬울 swiul	쉽던 swipdeon	쉬웠던 swiwotteon

Want	Can
–	쉬울 수 있어요 swiul su isseoyo

Don't (Imperative)	Whether or not		
–	쉬운지 swiunji	쉬웠는지 swiwonneunji	쉬울지 swiulji

(tell someone) that	(tell someone) to
쉽다고 swipdago	–

Sample Sentences

Track
15

1. 한국어는 정말 쉬워요.
   Korean is really easy.

2. 이게 제일 쉬운 방법이에요.
   This is the easiest way (method).

3. 이번 단어 시험이 쉬울지 안 쉬울지는 저도 모르겠어요.
   I'm not sure whether the vocabulary test will be easy or not.

4. 쉽다고 들었는데 하나도 안 쉬웠어요.
   I heard that it was easy, but it wasn't easy at all.

5. 스테파니 씨한테는 쉬울 거예요.
   It will be easy for Stephanie.

Quiz

1. 아랍어는 별로 안 (   ).
   Arabic is not that easy.

2. (   ) 들었는데 저한테는 정말 어려웠어요.
   I heard that it was easy, but it was really difficult for me.

3. 테리스 씨한테는 별로 안 (   ).
   It won't be that easy for Terris.

Answers :
1. 쉬워요 / 2. 쉽다고 / 3. 쉬울 거예요

어렵다
to be difficult,
to be hard, to be tough

Conjugation

어렵다
eo·ryeop·da

Present	*Past*	*Future / Guessing*	*Present Progressive*
어려워요	어려웠어요	어려울 거예요	–
eoryeowoyo	eoryeowosseoyo	eoryeoul geoyeyo	

Imperative

–   –   –

Modifier

어려운	–	어려울	어렵던	어려웠던
eoryeoun		eoryeoul	eoryeopdeon	eoryeowotteon

Want	*Can*
–	어려울 수 있어요
	eoryeoul su isseoyo

Don't (Imperative)	*Whether or not*		
–	어려운지	어려웠는지	어려울지
	eoryeounji	eoryeowonneunji	eoryeoulji

(tell someone) that	*(tell someone) to*
어렵다고	–
eoryeopdago	

Sample Sentences

1. 시험 어려웠어요?
   Was the test hard?

2. 중국어가 영어보다 어려워요.
   Chinese is harder than English.

3. 어려운 문제가 있으면 저한테 물어보세요.
   If there is a difficult problem, ask me about it.

4. 초등학생들한테는 어려울 거예요.
   It will be difficult for elementary school students.

5. 많이 어려워요?
   Is it very hard?

Quiz

1. 프랑스어가 한국어보다 (   ).
   French is harder than Korean.

2. (   ) 문제가 있으면 저 말고 경화 씨 한테 물어보세요.
   If there is a difficult problem, ask Kyung-hwa about it, not me.

3. 경은 씨한테는 (   ).
   It will be difficult for Kyeong-eun.

Answers :
1. 어려워요 / 2. 어려운 / 3. 어려울 거예요

눕다
to lie (down)

Conjugation

눕다
nup-da

Present	Past	Future / Guessing	Present Progressive
누워요 nuwoyo	누웠어요 nuwosseoyo	누울 거예요 nu-ul geoyeyo	눕고 있어요 nupgo isseoyo
			누워 있어요* nuwo isseoyo

Imperative

누우세요 nu-useyo	누워요 nuwoyo	누워 nuwo	누워라 nuwora

Modifier

누운 nu-un	눕는 numneun	누울 nu-ul	눕던 nupdeon	누웠던 nuwotteon

Want / Can

Want	Can
눕고 싶어요 nupgo sipeoyo	누울 수 있어요 nu-ul su isseoyo

Don't (Imperative) / Whether or not

Don't (Imperative)	Whether or not		
눕지 마세요 nupji maseyo	눕는지 numneunji	누웠는지 nuwonneunji	누울지 nu-ulji

(tell someone) that / (tell someone) to

(tell someone) that	(tell someone) to
눕는다고 numneundago	누우라고 nu-urago

*present status

The Korean Verbs Guide - Vol.1

Sample Sentences

1. 여기에는 눕지 마세요.
   Please don't lie down here.

2. 머리가 아프면 잠깐 누우세요.
   If your head hurts, lie down for a little while.

3. 여기 두 명 누울 수 있어요?
   Can two people lie down here?

4. 아직도 누워 있어요?
   Are you still lying down?

5. 지금 자려고 누웠어요.
   I'm lying down trying to go to sleep.

Quiz

1. 그쪽에는 (   ).
   Please don't lie down over there.

2. 다리를 다쳤으면 여기 (   ).
   If you hurt your legs, please lie down here.

3. 거기 어른 다섯 명이 (   )?
   Can five adults lie down there?

Answers :
1. 눕지 마세요 / 2. 누우세요 / 3. 누울 수 있어요

너무 추워요.

It's really cold.

춥다
to be cold;
to feel cold

Conjugation

춥다
chup-da

Present	Past	Future / Guessing	Present Progressive
추워요 chuwoyo	추웠어요 chuwosseoyo	추울 거예요 chuul geoyeyo	–

Imperative			
–	–	–	–

Modifier				
추운 chu-un	–	추울 chu-ul	춥던 chupdeon	추웠던 chuwotteon

Want	Can
–	추울 수 있어요 chu-ul su isseoyo

Don't (Imperative)	Whether or not		
–	추운지 chu-unji	추웠는지 chuwonneunji	추울지 chu-ulji

(tell someone) that	(tell someone) to
춥다고 chupdago	–

Sample Sentences

1. 러시아는 겨울에 정말 춥다고 들었어요.
   I heard winters in Russia are really cold.

2. 작년 크리스마스에 얼마나 추웠는지 기억이 안 나요.
   I don't remember how cold it was last Christmas.

3. 너무 추워요.
   It's really cold.

4. 올 겨울은 작년보다 더 추울 거예요.
   This winter is going to be colder than last year's.

5. 저는 추운 날에는 방에서 따뜻한 핫초코를 마시는 걸 좋아해요.
   I like drinking warm hot chocolate in my room on cold days.

Quiz

1. 주영 씨가 사는 곳은 겨울에 정말 (   ) 들었어요.
   I heard it's really cold where Juyoung lives.

2. 작년 겨울에 얼마나 (   ) 기억나는 사람 있어요?
   Is there anyone who remembers how cold it was last winter?

3. 저는 (   ) 날에는 방에서 자는 걸 좋아해요.
   I like sleeping in my room on cold days.

Answers :
1. 춥다고 / 2. 추웠는지 / 3. 추운

덥다

to be hot;
to feel hot

Conjugation

덥다
deop-da

Present	Past	Future / Guessing	Present Progressive
더워요	더웠어요	더울 거예요	–
deowoyo	deowosseoyo	deoul geoyeyo	

Imperative

–	–	–	–

Modifier

더운	–	더울	덥던	더웠던
deoun		deoul	deopdeon	deowotteon

Want	Can
–	더울 수 있어요
	deoul su isseoyo

Don't (Imperative)	Whether or not		
–	더운지	더웠는지	더울지
	deounji	deowonneunji	deoulji

(tell someone) that	(tell someone) to
덥다고	–
deopdago	

83

Sample Sentences

1. 내년 여름은 더 더울 거예요.
   Next year, it's going to be even hotter during the summertime.

2. 건물 안은 춥고, 밖은 더워요.
   Inside the building it is cold, and outside it is hot.

3. 싱가포르는 아주 덥다고 들었어요.
   I heard that the weather in Singapore is really hot.

4. 한국의 여름이 이렇게 더운지 몰랐어요.
   I didn't know summer in Korea was this hot.

5. 더운 나라에서 온 사람들은 한국의 겨울이 너무 힘들대요.
   People who come from countries with warm climates say Korean
   winters are very tough.

Quiz

1. 다음주부터 (   ).
   Starting from next week, it's going to be hot.

2. 지아 씨가 사는 곳은 (   ) 들었어요.
   I heard that the weather where Ji-ah is living is hot.

3. (   ) 나라에서 온 친구들은 모두 이곳의 겨울이 너무 춥대요.
   My friends who come from countries with warm climates, say winter
   here is too cold.

Answers :
1. 더울 거예요 / 2. 덥다고 / 3. 더운

귀엽다
to be cute

Conjugation

Present	Past	Future / Guessing	Present Progressive
귀여워요	귀여웠어요	귀여울 거예요	–
gwiyeowoyo	gwiyeowosseoyo	gwiyeoul geoyeyo	

		Imperative	
–	–	–	–

		Modifier		
귀여운	–	귀여울	귀엽던	귀여웠던
gwiyeoun		gwiyeoul	gwiyeopdeon	gwiyeowotteon

Want	Can
–	귀여울 수 있어요
	gwiyeoul su isseoyo

Don't (Imperative)	Whether or not		
–	귀여운지	귀여웠는지	귀여울지
	gwiyeounji	gwiyeowonneunji	gwiyeoulji

(tell someone) that	(tell someone) to
귀엽다고	–
gwiyeopdago	

Sample Sentences

Track 19

1. 귀여운 인형을 사고 싶어요.
   I want to buy a cute doll.

2. 이 치마 입으면 정말 귀여울 거예요.
   If you wear this skirt, you will look really cute.

3. 오늘 누가 저한테 귀엽다고 했어요.
   Someone told me that I was cute today.

4. 아까 본 강아지 정말 귀여웠어요.
   The puppy that we saw a little while ago was really cute.

5. 리카 씨는 웃을 때 참 귀여워요.
   Rika is really cute when she smiles.

Quiz

1. (   ) 모자를 빌리고 싶어요.
   I want to borrow a cute hat.

2. 저 강아지 인형을 들고 사진을 찍으면 정말 (   ).
   If you take a photo holding that stuffed puppy, you will look really cute.

3. 지난주에 동물원에서 본 새끼 얼룩말 정말 (   ).
   The baby zebra we saw last week was really cute.

Answers :
1. 귀여운 / 2. 귀여울 거예요 / 3. 귀여웠어요

87

싫다
to not like,
to hate; to not want

Conjugation

싫다
sil-ta

Present	Past	Future / Guessing	Present Progressive
싫어요	싫었어요	–	–
sireoyo	sireosseoyo		

Imperative

–	–	–	–

Modifier

싫은	–	싫을	싫던	싫었던
sireun		si-reul	silteon	sireotteon

Want	Can
–	싫을 수 있어요
	sireul su isseoyo

Don't (Imperative)	Whether or not
–	싫은지 · 싫었는지 · 싫을지
	sireunji · sireonneunji · sireulji

(tell someone) that	(tell someone) to
싫다고	–
siltago	

Sample Sentences

1. 저는 봄이 제일 좋고 여름이 제일 싫어요.
   I like spring the best, and hate summer the most.

2. 싫다고 말했는데, 무시당했어요.
   I said I didn't like it, but I was ignored.

3. 지금은 괜찮은데 옛날에는 비가 정말 싫었어요.
   Right now it's okay, but I really used to hate rain.

4. 싫은 음식은 안 먹어도 돼요.
   You don't have to eat foods you don't like.

5. 왜 싫은지 말해줄 수 있어요?
   Can you tell me why you don't like it?

Quiz

1. 저는 노는 게 제일 좋고 공부하는 게 제일 (   ).
   I like playing the best, and hate studying the most.

2. (   ) 게임은 안 해도 돼요.
   You don't have to play games you don't like.

3. 뭐가 (   ) 물어봐 줄 수 있어요?
   Can you ask him what he doesn't like about it?

Answers :
1. 싫어요 / 2. 싫은 / 3. 싫은지

지금 찾고 있어요.

I'm looking for it now.

찾다

to look for, to search; to find

Conjugation

찾다
chat-da

Present	Past	Future / Guessing	Present Progressive
찾아요	찾았어요	찾을 거예요	찾고 있어요
chajayo	chajasseoyo	chajeul geoyeyo	chatgo isseoyo

Imperative

찾으세요	찾아요	찾아	찾아라
chajeuseyo	chajayo	chaja	chajara

Modifier

찾은	찾는	찾을	찾던	찾았던
chajeun	channeun	chajeul	chatteon	chajatteon

Want	Can
찾고 싶어요	찾을 수 있어요
chatgo sipeoyo	chajeul su isseoyo

Don't (Imperative)		Whether or not	
찾지 마세요	찾는지	찾았는지	찾을지
chatji maseyo	channeunji	chajanneunji	chajeulji

(tell someone) that	(tell someone) to
찾는다고	찾으라고
channeundago	chajeurago

Sample Sentences

1. 지금 찾고 있어요.
   I'm looking for it now.

2. 찾았어요?
   Have you found it?

3. 어떻게 찾았어요?
   How did you find it?

4. 찾는 물건이 있으면 저한테 말씀해 주세요.
   If you are looking for anything, please tell me.

5. 어디서 찾았는지 말해 주세요.
   Please tell me where you found it.

Quiz

1. 석진 씨가 (   ).
   Seokjin is looking for it now.

2. 어디서 (   )?
   Where did you find it?

3. 누가 (   ) 알아요?
   Do you know who found it?

Answers :
1. 찾고 있어요 / 2. 찾았어요 / 3. 찾았는지

입다

to wear,
to put on

Conjugation

입다
ip-da

Present	Past	Future / Guessing	Present Progressive
입어요	입었어요	입을 거예요	입고 있어요
ibeoyo	ibeosseoyo	ibeul geoyeyo	ipgo isseoyo

Imperative

입으세요	입어요	입어	입어라
ibeuseyo	ibeoyo	ibeo	ibeora

Modifier

입은	입는	입을	입던	입었던
ibeun	imneun	ibeul	ipdeon	ibeotteon

Want	Can
입고 싶어요	입을 수 있어요
ipgo sipeoyo	ibeul su isseoyo

Don't (Imperative)	Whether or not		
입지 마세요	입는지	입었는지	입을지
ipji maseyo	imneunji	ibeonneunji	ibeulji

(tell someone) that	(tell someone) to
입는다고	입으라고
imneundago	ibeurago

The Korean Verbs Guide - Vol.1

Sample Sentences

1. 오늘 뭐 입을 거예요?
   What are you going to wear today?

2. 저는 지금 반바지를 입고 있어요.
   I'm wearing shorts right now.

3. 내일 뭐 입을지 아직 모르겠어요.
   I'm still not sure what I am going to wear tomorrow.

4. 오늘 추우니까 따뜻하게 입으세요.
   Since it's cold today, please make sure to wear warm clothes.

5. 오늘 제가 입을 옷이에요. 어때요?
   These are the clothes I will wear today. What do you think?

Quiz

1. 내일 결혼식에서 뭐 (   )?
   What are you going to wear at the wedding tomorrow?

2. 효진 씨는 지금 원피스를 (   ).
   Hyojin is wearing a dress right now.

3. 오늘 많이 걸을 거니까 편한 옷 (   ).
   Since we are going to walk a lot today, please make sure to wear comfortable clothes.

잡다

to grab, to hold;
to catch (the opportunity)

Conjugation

잡다
jap-da

Present	Past	Future / Guessing	Present Progressive
잡아요	잡았어요	잡을 거예요	잡고 있어요
jabayo	jabasseoyo	jabeul geoyeyo	japgo isseoyo

Imperative

잡으세요	잡아요	잡아	잡아라
jabeuseyo	jabayo	jaba	jabara

Modifier

잡은	잡는	잡을	잡던	잡았던
jabeun	jamneun	jabeul	japdeon	jabatteon

Want

잡고 싶어요
japgo sipeoyo

Can

잡을 수 있어요
jabeul su isseoyo

Don't (Imperative)

잡지 마세요
japji maseyo

Whether or not

잡는지	잡았는지	잡을지
jamneunji	jabanneunji	jabeulji

(tell someone) that

잡는다고
jamneundago

(tell someone) to

잡으라고
jabeurago

Sample Sentences

1. 누가 잡았어요?
   Who caught it?

2. 내가 공 던질 테니까 잡아.
   I'm going to throw the ball, so catch it.

3. 석진 씨가 잡고 있어요.
   Seokjin is holding it.

4. 범인을 제가 잡을 거예요.
   I am going to catch the criminal.

5. 누가 범인을 잡았는지 아세요?
   Do you know who caught the criminal?

Quiz

1. 경화 씨가 양손으로 (   ).
   Kyung-hwa is holding it with both hands.

2. 저 모기는 테리스 씨가 (   ).
   Terris is going to catch that mosquito.

3. 경찰이 어디서 그 사람을 (   ) 아세요?
   Do you know where the police caught him?

Answers :
1. 잡고 있어요 / 2. 잡을 거예요 / 3. 잡았는지

The Korean Verbs Guide - Vol.1

열다
to open

Conjugation

열다
yeol-da

	Present	Past	Future / Guessing	Present Progressive
	열어요	열었어요	열 거예요	열고 있어요
	yeoreoyo	yeoreosseoyo	yeol geoyeyo	yeolgo isseoyo

Imperative

여세요	열어요	열어	열어라
yeoseyo	yeoreoyo	yeoreo	yeoreora

Modifier

연	여는	열	열던	열었던
yeon	yeoneun	yeol	yeoldeon	yeoreotteon

Want / Can

Want		Can	
열고 싶어요		열 수 있어요	
yeolgo sipeoyo		yeol su isseoyo	

Don't (Imperative) / Whether or not

Don't (Imperative)	Whether or not		
열지 마세요	여는지	열었는지	열지
yeolji maseyo	yeoneunji	yeoreonneunji	yeolji

(tell someone) that / (tell someone) to

(tell someone) that	(tell someone) to
연다고	열라고
yeondago	yeollago

The Korean Verbs Guide - Vol.1

Sample Sentences

1. 이 창문 누가 열었어요?
   Who opened this window?

2. 벌레가 들어올지도 모르니까 창문 열지 마세요.
   Bugs might come in, so please do not open the window.

3. 한 손으로 열 수 있어요.
   I can open it with one hand.

4. 창문 누가 열었는지 알아요?
   Do you know who opened the window?

5. 지금 이 시간에 문 연 가게는 없을 거예요.
   There must be no shops open at this hour.

Quiz

1. 냄비 뚜껑 언제 (   )?
   When did you open the lid of the pot?

2. 추우니까 문 (   ).
   It's cold, so please don't open the door.

3. 저 혼자서 (   ).
   I can open it by myself.

놀라다

to be surprised;
to be shocked

Conjugation

Present	Past	Future / Guessing	Present Progressive
놀라요	놀랐어요	놀랄 거예요	놀라고 있어요
nollayo	nollasseoyo	nollal geoyeyo	nollago isseoyo

Imperative

–	–	–	–

Modifier

놀란	놀라는	놀랄	놀라던	놀랐던
nollan	nollaneun	nollal	nolladeon	nollatteon

Want	Can
–	놀랄 수 있어요
	nollal su isseoyo

Don't (Imperative)	Whether or not		
놀라지 마세요	놀라는지	놀랐는지	놀랄지
nollaji maseyo	nollaneunji	nollanneunji	nollalji

(tell someone) that	(tell someone) to
놀란다고	놀라라고
nollandago	nollarago

Sample Sentences

1. 놀라는 모습이 귀여웠어요.
   The way you were startled was cute.

2. 놀라지 마세요.
   Don't be surprised.

3. 제가 얼마나 놀랐는지 아세요?
   Do you know how surprised I was?

4. 뭘 보고 그렇게 놀랐어요?
   What did you see that shocked you so much?

5. 왜 그렇게 놀란 표정 짓고 있어요?
   Why do you have such a shocked look on your face ?

The Korean Verbs Guide - Vol.1

Quiz

1. 지훈 씨는 (   ) 모습이 웃겨요.
   The way Jihoon gets startled is funny.

2. 이거 보고 (   ).
   Don't be surprised after you see this, please.

3. 수연 씨가 왜 그렇게 (   ) 표정을 짓고 있었는지 알아요?
   Do you know why Sooyeon has such a shocked look on her face?

Answers :
1. 놀라는 / 2. 놀라지 마세요 / 3. 놀란

왜 갑자기 멈췄어요?

Why did you suddenly stop?

멈추다
to stop;
something stops

Conjugation

멈추다
meom-chu-da

Present	Past	Future / Guessing	Present Progressive
멈춰요	멈췄어요	멈출 거예요	멈추고 있어요
meomchweoyo	meomchweosseoyo	meomchul geoyeyo	meomchugo isseoyo

Imperative

멈추세요	멈춰요	멈춰	멈춰라
meomchuseyo	meomchwoyo	meomchwo	meomchwora

Modifier

멈춘	멈추는	멈출	멈추던	멈췄던
meomchun	meomchuneun	meomchul	meomchudeon	meomchwotteon

Want

멈추고 싶어요	멈출 수 있어요
meomchugo sipeoyo	meomchul su isseoyo

Can

Don't (Imperative)

멈추지 마세요	멈추는지	멈췄는지	멈출지
meomchuji maseyo	meomchuneunji	meomchwonneunji	meomchulji

Whether or not

(tell someone) that

멈춘다고	멈추라고
meomchundago	meomchurago

(tell someone) to

Sample Sentences

1. 언제든지 멈출 수 있어요.
   I can stop at any time.

2. 시계가 자꾸 멈춘다고 들었어요.
   I heard your watch keeps stopping.

3. 이 버튼을 누르면 음악을 멈출 수 있어요.
   If you press this button, you can stop the music.

4. 이 기계가 언제 멈췄는지 아세요?
   Do you know when this machine stopped?

5. 공사를 멈추라고 말해 주세요.
   Please tell them to stop the construction.

Quiz

1. 누구든지 쉽게 (   ).
   Anyone can stop this easily.

2. 자동차가 도로에서 자꾸 (   ) 들었어요.
   I heard your car keeps stopping on the road.

3. 경은 씨 컴퓨터가 왜 (   ) 아세요?
   Do you know why Kyeong-eun's computer stopped?

Answers :
1. 멈출 수 있어요 / 2. 멈춘다고 / 3. 멈췄는지

The Korean Verbs Guide - Vol.1

고르다

to choose, to pick

Conjugation

Present	Past	Future / Guessing	Present Progressive
골라요	골랐어요	고를 거예요	고르고 있어요
gollayo	gollaseoyo	goreul geoyeyo	goreugo isseoyo

Imperative

고르세요	골라요	골라	골라라
goreuseyo	gollayo	golla	gollara

Modifier

고른	고르는	고를	고르던	골랐던
goreun	goreuneun	goreul	goreudeon	gollatteon

Want

고르고 싶어요
goreugo sipeoyo

Can

고를 수 있어요
goreul su isseoyo

Don't (Imperative)

고르지 마세요
goreuji maseyo

Whether or not

고르는지	골랐는지	고를지
goreuneunji	gollanneunji	goreulji

(tell someone) that

고른다고
goreundago

(tell someone) to

고르라고
goreurago

Sample Sentences

Track 28

1. 원하는 색깔을 고를 수 있어요.
   You can pick the color you want.

2. 그건 고르지 마세요.
   Please don't pick that one.

3. 제가 고른 옷이 마음에 안 드세요?
   You don't like the clothes I picked?

4. 지금 고르고 있어요.
   I am choosing (something) right now.

5. 엄마가 다 고른다고 하셨어요.
   My mom said she would pick everything.

Quiz

1. 좋아하는 그림을 (   ).
   You can pick a painting you like.

2. 테이블 위에 있는 건 (   ).
   Please don't choose the one on the table.

3. 서진 씨가 (   ) 신발이 마음에 드세요?
   Do you like the shoes Seojin picked?

Answers :
1. 고를 수 있어요 / 2. 고르지 마세요 / 3. 고른

모르다
to not know

Conjugation

모르다
mo-reu-da

Present	Past	Future / Guessing	Present Progressive
몰라요	몰랐어요	모를 거예요	모르고 있어요
mollayo	mollasseoyo	moreul geoyeyo	moreugo isseoyo

Imperative

– – – –

Modifier

모른	모르는	모를	모르던	몰랐던
moreun	moreuneun	moreul	moreudeon	mollatteon

Want	Can
–	모를 수 있어요
	moreul su isseoyo

Don't (Imperative)	Whether or not		
–	모르는지	몰랐는지	모를지
	moreuneunji	mollanneunji	moreulji

(tell someone) that	(tell someone) to
모른다고	–
moreundago	

Sample Sentences

1. 테리스는 너무 어려서 모를 거예요.
   Terris is too young, so he won't know.

2. 그 사건에 대해 잘 모르는 사람은 아무 말도 하지 마세요.
   People who don't know well about this case, please do not say anything.

3. 어떻게 모를 수 있어요?
   How can you not know?

4. 모른다고 거짓말하지 마세요.
   Please don't lie saying you don't know.

5. 경화 씨가 그걸 아는지 모르는지 모르겠어요.
   I don't know if Kyeong-hwa knows it or not.

The Korean Verbs Guide - Vol.1

Quiz

1. 선미 씨는 외국에서 오래 살아서 (   ).
   Seonmi lived abroad for a long time, so she won't know.

2. 제가 지금 무슨 말을 하는지 (   ) 사람은 손을 드세요.
   People who don't know what I'm talking about now, please raise
   your hand.

3. 연재 씨가 그걸 아는지 (   ) 물어봐 주세요.
   Please ask Yeonjae if she knows or not.

Answers :
1. 모를 거예요 / 2. 모르는 / 3. 모르는지

빠르다
to be fast,
to be quick

Conjugation

ppa-reu-da

Present	Past	Future / Guessing	Present Progressive
빨라요	빨랐어요	빠를 거예요	–
ppallayo	ppallasseoyo	ppareul geoyeyo	

Imperative			
–	–	–	–

Modifier				
빠른	–	빠를	빠르던	빨랐던
ppareun		ppareul	ppareudeon	ppallatteon

Want	Can
–	빠를 수 있어요
	ppareul su isseoyo

Don't (Imperative)	Whether or not		
–	빠른지	빨랐는지	빠를지
	ppareunji	ppallanneunji	ppareulji

(tell someone) that	(tell someone) to
빠르다고	–
ppareudago	

The Korean Verbs Guide - Vol.1

118

Sample Sentences

1. 전화로 연락하는 게 빠를 거예요.
   Calling her would be quicker.

2. 제가 조금 더 빨랐어요.
   I was a little faster.

3. 한국은 인터넷 속도가 굉장히 빠르다고 들었어요.
   I heard that the Internet speed in Korea is really fast.

4. 토끼가 거북이보다 빨라요.
   Rabbits are faster than turtles.

5. 오토바이가 그렇게 빠를지 몰랐어요.
   I didn't know that motorcycles were that fast.

Quiz

1. 직접 얘기하는 게 (   ).
   Talking to him in person would be quicker.

2. 그렇게 (   ) 자동차가 어디 있어요?
   There is no car that fast .

3. 제 핸드폰이 미키 씨 핸드폰보다 (   ).
   My cellphone is faster than yours, Miki.

Answers :
1. 빠를 거예요 / 2. 빠른 / 3. 빨라요

119

작년에 산책하면서
많이 걸었던 길이에요.

This is a road that I walked on a lot last year.

걷다

to walk

Conjugation

geot-da

	Present	Past	Future / Guessing	Present Progressive
	걸어요	걸었어요	걸을 거예요	걷고 있어요
	georeoyo	georeosseoyo	gereul geoyeyo	geotgo isseoyo

Imperative

걸으세요	걸어요	걸어	걸어라
georeuseyo	georeoyo	georeo	georeora

Modifier

걸은	걷는	걸을	걷던	걸었던
georeun	geonneun	georeul	geotteon	georeotteon

Want / Can

Want	Can
걷고 싶어요	걸을 수 있어요
geotgo sipeoyo	georeul su isseoyo

Don't (Imperative) / Whether or not

Don't (Imperative)	Whether or not		
걷지 마세요	걷는지	걸었는지	걸을지
geotji maseyo	geonneunji	georeonneunji	georeulji

(tell someone) that / (tell someone) to

(tell someone) that	(tell someone) to
걷는다고	걸으라고
geonneundago	georeurago

The Korean Verbs Guide - Vol.1

Sample Sentences

1. 하루에 몇시간 걸어요?
   How many hours do you walk a day?

2. 소리내면서 걷지 마세요.
   Please don't make sounds while you walk.

3. 작년에 산책하면서 많이 걸었던 길이에요.
   This is a road that I walked on a lot last year.

4. 살 빼고 싶으면 많이 걸으세요.
   If you want to lose weight, please walk a lot.

5. 지난주에 얼마나 걸었는지 모르겠어요.
   I don't know how much I walked last week.

Quiz

1. 그쪽 길에서는 (   ).
   Please don't walk on the road over there.

2. 살 빼려고 운동할 때 많이 (   ) 길이에요.
   This is a road that I walked on a lot when I exercised to lose weight.

3. 이번 여행에서 우리가 얼마나 (   ) 알아요?
   Do you know how much we walked during this trip?

Answers :
1. 걷지 마세요 / 2. 걸었던 or 걸은 / 3. 걸었는지

123

자르다
to cut

Conjugation

자르다
ja-reu-da

Present	Past	Future / Guessing	Present Progressive
잘라요	잘랐어요	자를 거예요	자르고 있어요
jallayo	jallasseoyo	jareul geoyeyo	jareugo isseoyo

Imperative

자르세요	잘라요	잘라	잘라라
jareuseyo	jallayo	jalla	jallara

Modifier

자른	자르는	자를	자르던	잘랐던
jareun	jareuneun	jareul	jareudeon	jallatteon

Want

자르고 싶어요
jareugo sipeoyo

Can

자를 수 있어요
jareul su isseoyo

Don't (Imperative)

자르지 마세요
jareuji maseyo

Whether or not

자르는지	잘랐는지	자를지
jareuneunji	jallanneunji	jareulji

(tell someone) that

자른다고
jareundago

(tell someone) to

자르라고
jareurago

Sample Sentences

1. 제가 실수로 이 선을 잘랐어요.
   I cut this cord by accident.

2. 과일을 자르고 있어요.
   I'm cutting fruits.

3. 그렇게 머리를 짧게 자른 이유가 뭐예요?
   What is the reason you cut your hair so short?

4. 선생님이 머리 자르라고 하셨어요.
   The teacher told me to cut my hair.

5. 머리 잘랐는지 몰랐어요.
   I didn't know you cut your hair.

Quiz

1. 준석 씨가 일부러 이 종이를 (   ).
   Joonseok cut this paper on purpose.

2. 마우스 선을 (   ) 이유가 뭐예요?
   What is the reason you cut the mouse cord?

3. 수영 씨가 (   ) 몰랐어요?
   You didn't know Su-young cut it?

Answers :
1. 잘랐어요 / 2. 자른 / 3. 잘랐는지

The Korean Verbs Guide - Vol.1

다르다

to be different

Conjugation

다르다
da-reu-da

Present	Past	Future / Guessing	Present Progressive
달라요	달랐어요	다를 거예요	–
dallayo	dallasseoyo	dareul geoyeyo	

Imperative

–	–	–	–

Modifier

다른	–	다를	다르던	달랐던
dareun		dareul	dareudeon	dallatteon

Want	Can
–	다를 수 있어요
	dareul su isseoyo

Don't (Imperative)	Whether or not		
–	다른지	달랐는지	다를지
	dareunji	dallanneunji	dareulji

(tell someone) that	(tell someone) to
다르다고	–
dareudago	

Sample Sentences

1. 다른 사람이 된 것 같아요.
   It seems like he's become a different person.

2. 지금까지하고는 많이 다를 거예요.
   Things are going to be very different from how it was until now.

3. 지역에 따라 요금이 조금씩 다를 수 있어요.
   Fees may be different, depending on the region.

4. 뭐가 달라요?
   What is different?

5. 뭐가 다른지 모르겠어요.
   I don't know what's different.

Quiz

1. 어제하고 조금 (   ).
   It's going to be a little different from yesterday.

2. 사람에 따라 의견이 (   ).
   Opinions can be different, depending on the person.

3. 어디가 (   ) 알겠어요?
   Can you tell where is different?

듣다
to listen, to hear

Conjugation

듣다
deut-da

Present	Past	Future / Guessing	Present Progressive
들어요	들었어요	들을 거예요	듣고 있어요
deureoyo	deureosseoyo	deureul geoyeyo	deutgo isseoyo

Imperative

들으세요	들어요	들어	들어라
deureuseyo	deureoyo	deureo	deureora

Modifier

들은	듣는	들을	듣던	들었던
deureun	deunneun	deureul	deutteon	deureotteon

Want	Can
듣고 싶어요	들을 수 있어요
deutgo sipeoyo	deureul su isseoyo

Don't (Imperative)	Whether or not		
듣지 마세요	듣는지	들었는지	들을지
deutji maseyo	deunneunji	deureonneunji	deureulji

(tell someone) that	(tell someone) to
듣는다고	들으라고
deunneundago	deureurago

Sample Sentences

1. 중학교 때 많이 듣던 노래예요.
   This is a song I used to listen to a lot in middle school.

2. 잘 들어.
   Listen carefully.
   Listen up.

3. 듣고 있어요.
   I'm listening.

4. 음악 듣고 싶어요.
   I want to listen to music.

5. 제 말을 듣는 사람이 한명도 없네요.
   There is not even one person listening to what I'm saying.

Quiz

1. 제 동생이 어릴 때 많이 (   ) 동요예요.
   This is a children's song my little sister used to listen to a lot when she was little.

2. 저도 똑같은 음악 (   ).
   I'm listening to the same music.

3. 소녀시대 노래를 (   ).
   I want to listen to SNSD's songs.

Answers :
1. 듣던 / 2. 듣고 있어요 / 3. 듣고 싶어요

The Korean Verbs Guide - Vol.1

물어보다
to ask

Conjugation

물어보다
mu-reo-bo-da

	Present	Past	Future / Guessing	Present Progressive
	물어봐요 mureobwayo	물어봤어요 mureobwasseoyo	물어볼 거예요 mureo bol geoyeyo	물어보고 있어요 mureobogo isseoyo

Imperative

물어보세요 mureoboseyo	물어봐요 mureobwayo	물어봐 mureobwa	물어봐라 mureobwara

Modifier

물어본 mureobon	물어보는 mureoboneun	물어볼 mureobol	물어보던 mureobodeon	물어봤던 mureobwatteon

Want / Can

Want	Can
물어보고 싶어요 mureobogo sipeoyo	물어볼 수 있어요 mureobol su isseoyo

Don't (Imperative) / Whether or not

Don't (Imperative)	Whether or not		
물어보지 마세요 mureoboji maseyo	물어보는지 mureoboneunji	물어봤는지 nureobwanneunji	물어볼지 mureobolji

(tell someone) that / (tell someone) to

(tell someone) that	(tell someone) to
물어본다고 mureobondago	물어보라고 mureoborago

The Korean Verbs Guide - Vol.1

Sample Sentences

1. 전화로 물어보세요.
   Please ask him over the phone.

2. 이거 물어봤던 사람이 누구죠?
   Who's the person who asked this?

3. 물어본 질문에만 답하세요.
   Please only answer the questions asked.

4. 언제 물어볼 거예요?
   When are you going to ask?

5. 뭐든지 물어보세요.
   Please ask me whatever.

Quiz

1. 궁금하면 직접 (   ).
   If you are curious, please ask him by yourself.

2. 지난주 수업 시간에 이거 (   ) 사람 누구인지 알아요?
   Do you know the person who asked this last week in class?

3. (   ) 질문에 다 답했어요?
   Did you answer all the questions asked?

Answers :
1. 물어보세요 or 물어보렴 / 2. 물어봤던 or 물어본 / 3. 물어본

웃는 얼굴이 예쁜 사람이
좋아요.

I like people with pretty smiles.

웃다
to laugh, to smile

Conjugation

ut-da

Present	Past	Future / Guessing	Present Progressive
웃어요	웃었어요	웃을 거예요	웃고 있어요
useoyo	useosseoyo	useul geoyeyo	utgo isseoyo

Imperative

웃으세요	웃어요	웃어	웃어라
useuseyo	useoyo	useo	useora

Modifier

웃은	웃는	웃을	웃던	웃었던
useun	unneun	useul	utteon	useotteon

Want	Can
웃고 싶어요	웃을 수 있어요
utgo sipeoyo	useul su isseoyo

Don't (Imperative)	Whether or not	
웃지 마세요	웃는지	웃었는지	웃을지
utji maseyo	unneunji	usseonneunnji	useulji

(tell someone) that	(tell someone) to
웃는다고	웃으라고
unneundago	useurago

The Korean Verbs Guide - Vol.1

Sample Sentences

Track
36

1. 우리 아기는 뽀로로를 보면 늘 웃어요.
   Our child smiles when he sees Pororo.

2. 웃는 얼굴이 예쁜 사람이 좋아요.
   I like people with pretty smiles.

3. 윤주 씨가 지금 왜 웃는지 저도 모르겠어요.
   I don't know why Yoonju is laughing now either.

4. 억지로라도 웃으세요.
   Even if it is forced, please smile

5. 지금 웃을 때가 아니에요.
   This is not the time to laugh.

Quiz

1. 이 광고가 TV에 나오면 우리 강아지는 늘 (   ).
   When this commercial is on TV, our puppy always smiles.

2. (   ) 얼굴이 귀여운 사람 좀 소개시켜 주세요.
   Please set me up with someone who has a cute smile.

3. 수연 씨가 왜 (   ) 알아요?
   Do you know why Sooyeong is laughing?

Answers :
1. 웃어요 / 2. 웃는 / 3. 웃는지

받다

to receive, to get, to accept

Conjugation

Present	Past	Future / Guessing	Present Progressive
받아요	받았어요	받을 거예요	받고 있어요
badayo	badasseoyo	badeul geoyeyo	batgo isseoyo

Imperative

받으세요	받아요	받아	받아라
badeuseyo	badayo	bada	badara

Modifier

받은	받는	받을	받던	받았던
badeun	banneun	badeul	batdeon	badatteon

Want	Can
받고 싶어요	받을 수 있어요
batgo sipeoyo	badeul su isseoyo

Don't (Imperative)	Whether or not		
받지 마세요	받는지	받았는지	받을지
batji maseyo	banneunji	badanneunji	badeulji

(tell someone) that	(tell someone) to
받는다고	받으라고
banneundago	badeurago

Sample Sentences

1. 저도 똑같은 거 받고 싶어요.
   I want to get the same thing.

2. 작년에 선물로 받았던 장난감이 망가졌어요.
   The toy that I got as a present last year broke.

3. 제가 던질 테니까 잘 받으세요.
   I'm going to throw it, so please catch it.

4. 언제 받았어요?
   When did you get it?

5. 제가 보낸 소포 잘 받았는지 확인하려고 전화했어요.
   I'm calling to see if you got the package I sent you.

Quiz

1. 이번 크리스마스에는 예쁜 장갑을 선물로 (   ).
   I want to get pretty gloves as a present.

2. 작년 생일에 스테파니 씨한테 (   ) 지갑을 잃어버렸어요.
   I lost the wallet that I got as a birthday present from Stephanie last year.

3. 지난주에 보낸 편지를 잘 (   ) 물어보세요.
   Please ask them if they got the letter we sent last week.

Answers :
1. 받고 싶어요 / 2. 받았던 or 받은 / 3. 받았는지

The Korean Verbs Guide - Vol.1

닫다
to close

Conjugation

Present	Past	Future / Guessing	Present Progressive
닫아요 dadayo	닫았어요 dadasseoyo	닫을 거예요 dadeul geoyeyo	닫고 있어요 datgo isseoyo

Imperative

닫으세요 dadeuseyo	닫아요 dadayo	닫아 dada	닫아라 dadara

Modifier

닫은 dadeun	닫는 danneun	닫을 dadeul	닫던 datdeon	닫았던 dadatteon

Want	Can
닫고 싶어요 datgo sipeoyo	닫을 수 있어요 dadeul su isseoyo

Don't (Imperative)	Whether or not		
닫지 마세요 datji maseyo	닫는지 danneunji	닫았는지 dadanneunji	닫을지 dadeulji

(tell someone) that	(tell someone) to
닫는다고 danneundago	닫으라고 dadeurago

Sample Sentences

Track
38

1. 그 가게 지난달에 문 닫았어요.
   That store closed down last month.

2. 나오면서 문을 닫았는지 안 닫았는지 기억이 안 나요.
   I don't remember if we closed the door or not while we were leaving.

3. 제가 올 때까지 문 닫지 마세요.
   Please don't close the door until I come.

4. 저희 식당은 매일 11시에 문 닫아요.
   Our restaurant closes every day at 11 o'clock.

5. 추워서 이제 창문 닫고 싶어요.
   It's cold now, so I want to close the window.

Quiz

1. 희철 씨한테 나올 때 창문 (   ) 안 (   ) 물어보세요.
   Please ask Heechul if he closed the window or not when he was leaving.

2. 동생이 집에 올 때까지 문 (   ).
   Please don't close the door until my little sister comes back home.

3. 이 가게는 토요일에는 새벽 2시에 문 (   ).
   This restaurant closes at 2 AM on Saturdays.

Answers :
1. 닫았는지, 닫았는지 / 2. 닫지 마세요 / 3. 닫아요

믿다

to believe (in),
to trust

Conjugation

믿다
mit-da

Present	Past	Future / Guessing	Present Progressive
믿어요	믿었어요	믿을 거예요	믿고 있어요
mideoyo	mideosseoyo	mideul geoyeyo	mitgo isseoyo

Imperative

믿으세요	믿어요	믿어	믿어라
mideuseyo	mideoyo	mideo	mideora

Modifier

믿은	믿는	믿을	믿던	믿었던
mideun	minneun	mideul	mitdeon	mideotteon

Want	Can
믿고 싶어요	믿을 수 있어요
mitgo sipeoyo	mideul su isseoyo

Don't (Imperative)	Whether or not	
믿지 마세요	믿는지	믿었는지 믿을지
mitji maseyo	minneunji	mideonneunji mideulji

(tell someone) that	(tell someone) to
믿는다고	믿으라고
minneundago	mideurago

Sample Sentences

1. 그걸 믿은 제가 바보였어요.
   I was a fool for believing that.

2. 사람들이 제 말을 믿을지 모르겠어요.
   I'm not sure if people will believe me.

3. 그 말을 지금 저보고 믿으라고요?
   You really expect me to believe what you just said?

4. 저는 정말 사장님만 믿었어요.
   I really only believed my boss.

5. 저는 그 사람을 끝까지 믿을 거예요.
   I'm going to believe that person until the end.

The Korean Verbs Guide - Vol.1

Quiz

1. 수정 씨 말을 (   ) 제가 잘못했어요.
   I was wrong for believing what Sujeong said.

2. 거짓말쟁이로 유명한 그 사람 말을 (   )요?
   You really expect me to believe what he, who is famous for being
   a liar, said?

3. 이번에는 지아 씨 말을 (   ).
   I'm going to believe what Ji-ah said this time.

Answers :
1. 믿은 / 2. 믿으라고 / 3. 믿을거예요

148

낫다

(regarding illness) to feel better, to recover; to be better

Conjugation

낫다
nat-da

Present	Past	Future / Guessing	Present Progressive
나아요	나았어요	나을 거예요	낫고 있어요
na-ayo	na-asseoyo	na-eul geoyeyo	nako isseoyo

Imperative

나으세요	나아요	나아	나아라
na-euseyo	na-ayo	na-a	na-ara

Modifier

나은	낫는	나을	낫던	나았던
na-eun	nanneun	na-eul	natteon	na-a-tteon

Want

낫고 싶어요	나을 수 있어요
natgo sipeoyo	na-eul su isseoyo

Can (above right)

Don't (Imperative)

낫지 마세요	낫는지	나았는지	나을지
natji maseyo	nannuenji	na-anneunji	na-eulji

Whether or not (above right)

(tell someone) that

낫는다고	나으라고
nanneundago	na-eurago

(tell someone) to (above right)

The Korean Verbs Guide - Vol.1

Sample Sentences

1. 빨리 나으세요.
   Get well soon.

2. 내일이면 다 나을 거예요.
   I will be all better by tomorrow.

3. 빨리 낫는 약 있어요?
   Is there any medicine that can make me get better quickly?

4. 운동하면 더 빨리 나을 수 있어요.
   You can get better quickly if you exercise.

5. 민수 씨는 병원에서 퇴원했다고는 했는데, 완전히 다 나았는지는 모르겠어요.
   I heard Minsoo got out of the hospital, but I'm not sure if he is fully recovered or not.

Quiz

1. 이 약 먹고 빨리 (   ).
   Take this pill and get well soon, please.

2. 감기 빨리 (   ) 방법 알아요?
   Do you know a method that can make me recover quickly from a cold?

3. 작년에 많이 아팠다고 들었는데 이제 다 (   ) 모르겠어요.
   I heard he was really sick last year, but I'm not sure if he recovered fully now or not.

Answers :
1. 나으세요 or 나아요 / 2. 낫는 / 3. 나았는지

씻다
to wash, to shower;
to freshen up

Conjugation

씻다
ssit-da

Present	*Past*	*Future / Guessing*	*Present Progressive*
씻어요	씻었어요	씻을 거예요	씻고 있어요
ssiseoyo	ssiseosseoyo	ssiseul geoyeyo	ssitgo isseoyo

Imperative

씻으세요	씻어요	씻어	씻어라
ssiseuseyo	ssiseoyo	ssiseo	ssiseora

Modifier

씻은	씻는	씻을	씻던	씻었던
ssiseun	ssinneun	ssiseul	ssitteon	ssiseotteon

Want	*Can*
씻고 싶어요	씻을 수 있어요
ssitgo sipeoyo	ssiseul su isseoyo

Don't (Imperative)	*Whether or not*		
씻지 마세요	씻는지	씻었는지	씻을지
ssitji maseyo	ssinneunji	ssiseonneunji	ssiseulji

(tell someone) that	*(tell someone) to*
씻는다고	씻으라고
ssinneundago	ssiseurago

Sample Sentences

1. 밥 먹기 전에 손 씻으세요.
   Please wash your hands before you eat.

2. 따뜻한 물로 씻고 싶어요.
   I want to shower with warm water.

3. 방금 씻은 사과 어디 있어요?
   Where is the apple that you just washed?

4. 제가 밥 먹기 전에 손을 씻었는지 안 씻었는지 기억이 안 나요.
   I don't remember if I washed my hands or not before I started eating.

5. 그 물 더러우니까 그 물로 씻지 마세요.
   That water is dirty, so don't use it (to wash up), please.

Quiz

1. 침대에 눕기 전에 발 (   ).
   Please wash your feet before you lie on the bed.

2. 자기 전에 뜨거운 물로 (   ).
   I want to shower with hot water before I go to bed.

3. 이 배를 먹기 전에 (   ) 안 (   ) 기억이 안 나요.
   I don't remember if I washed this pear or not before I ate it.

Answers :
1. 씻으세요 or 씻어요 / 2. 씻고 싶어요 / 3. 씻었는지, 씻었는지

The Korean Verbs Guide - Vol.1

피곤하면 여기 앉으세요.

If you are tired, please sit here.

앉다
to sit

Conjugation

Present	Past	Future / Guessing	Present Progressive
앉아요	앉았어요	앉을 거예요	앉고 있어요
anjayo	anjasseoyo	anjeul geoyeyo	an-kko isseoyo
			앉아 있어요*
			anja isseoyo

Imperative

앉으세요	앉아요	앉아	앉아라
anjeuseyo	anjayo	anja	anjara

Modifier

앉은	앉는	앉을	앉던	앉았던
anjeun	anneun	anjeul	andeon	anjatteon

Want

앉고 싶어요
an-kko sipeoyo

Can

앉을 수 있어요
anjeul su isseoyo

Don't (Imperative)

앉지 마세요
anji maseyo

Whether or not

앉는지	앉았는지	앉을지
anneunji	anjanneunji	anjeulji

(tell someone) that

앉는다고
anneundago

(tell someone) to

앉으라고
anjeurago

*present status

Sample Sentences

1. 뒷자리에 앉고 싶어요.
   I want to sit in the backseat.

2. 이 의자에 세 사람 앉을 수 있어요.
   Three people can sit on this chair.

3. 여기 누가 앉는지 알아요?
   Do you know who sits here?

4. 여기 앉을 거예요?
   Are you going to sit here?

5. 그런 자세로 앉지 마세요.
   Don't sit with that posture.

Quiz

1. 혼자 (   ).
   I want to sit by myself.

2. 이 컴퓨터 앞에는 누가 (   ) 알려주세요.
   Please tell me who sits in front of this computer.

3. 정말로 혼자 (   )?
   Are you really going to sit by yourself?

Answers :
1. 앉고 싶어요 / 2. 앉는지 / 3. 앉을 거예요

The Korean Verbs Guide - Vol.1

벗다
to take off,
to undress

Conjugation

벗다
beot-da

Present	Past	Future / Guessing	Present Progressive
벗어요	벗었어요	벗을 거예요	벗고 있어요
beoseoyo	beoseosseoyo	beoseul geoyeyo	beotgo isseoyo

Imperative

벗으세요	벗어요	벗어	벗어라
beoseuseyo	beoseoyo	beoseo	beoseora

Modifier

벗은	벗는	벗을	벗던	벗었던
beoseun	beonneun	beoseul	beotteon	beosseotteon

Want / Can

Want	Can
벗고 싶어요	벗을 수 있어요
beotgo sipeoyo	beoseul su isseoyo

Don't (Imperative) / Whether or not

Don't (Imperative)	Whether or not		
벗지 마세요	벗는지	벗었는지	벗을지
beotji maseyo	beonneunji	beoseonneunji	beoseulji

(tell someone) that / (tell someone) to

(tell someone) that	(tell someone) to
벗는다고	벗으라고
beonneundago	beoseurago

The Korean Verbs Guide - Vol.1

Sample Sentences

1. 실내에서는 선글라스 벗으세요.
   Please take off your sunglasses while you are inside.

2. 옷이 많이 젖어서 벗을 거예요.
   My clothes got wet, so I'm going to take them off.

3. 영화관에서 신발 벗지 마세요.
   Please don't take off your shoes in the movie theater.

4. 너무 답답해서 모자 벗었어요.
   I was feeling stuffy, so I took off my hat.

5. 저희 아이도 이제 혼자 옷을 입고 벗을 수 있어요.
   Our child can now put on and take off his clothes by himself.

Quiz

1. 교실안에서는 모자 (   ).
   Please take off your hat while you are in the classroom.

2. 자켓이 더러워져서 (   ).
   My jacket got dirty, so I'm going to take it off.

3. 카페 안이 더워서 자켓을 (   ).
   Inside the café was hot, so I took off my jacket.

Answers :
1. 벗으세요 or 벗어요 / 2. 벗을 거예요 / 3. 벗었어요

161

보내다
to send

Conjugation

보내다
bo·nae·da

Present	Past	Future / Guessing	Present Progressive
보내요	보냈어요	보낼 거예요	보내고 있어요
bonaeyo	bonaesseoyo	bonael geoyeyo	bonaego isseoyo

Imperative

보내세요	보내요	보내	보내라
bonaeseyo	bonaeyo	bonae	bonaera

Modifier

보낸	보내는	보낼	보내던	보냈던
bonaen	bonaeneun	bonael	bonaedeon	bonaetteon

Want

보내고 싶어요
bonaego sipeoyo

Can

보낼 수 있어요
bonael su isseoyo

Don't (Imperative)

보내지 마세요
bonaeji maseyo

Whether or not

보내는지	보냈는지	보낼지
bonaeneunji	bonaenneunji	bonaelji

(tell someone) that

보낸다고
bonaendago

(tell someone) to

보내라고
bonaerago

Sample Sentences

1. 어제 외국에 사는 친구한테 작은 선물을 보냈어요.
   I sent a small gift to my friend living abroad yesterday.

2. 저한테 보내세요.
   Please send it to me.

3. 누가 보냈는지 알 수 있어요?
   Can you let me know who sent it?

4. 누구를 보낼지 아직 안 정했어요.
   We haven't decided who we are going to send yet.

5. 친구가 오늘 보낸다고 했으니까 모레쯤 받을 수 있을 거예요.
   My friend said he would send it today, so I should get it the day after tomorrow.

Quiz

1. 지난달에 아기를 낳은 친구에게 선물을 (   ).
   I sent a present to my friend who had a baby last month.

2. 언제 (   ) 알려주세요.
   Please tell me when you sent it.

3. 뭐 (   ) 정했어요?
   Have you decided what you are going to send?

Answers :
1. 보냈어요 / 2. 보냈는지 / 3. 보낼지

팔다

to sell

Conjugation

Present	Past	Future / Guessing	Present Progressive
팔아요	팔았어요	팔 거예요	팔고 있어요
parayo	parasseoyo	pal geoyeyo	palgo isseoyo

Imperative

파세요	팔아요	팔아	팔아라
paseyo	parayo	para	parara

Modifier

판	파는	팔	팔던	팔았던
pan	paneun	pal	paldeon	paratteon

Want

Want	Can
팔고 싶어요	팔 수 있어요
palgo sipeoyo	pal su isseoyo

Don't (Imperative) / Whether or not

Don't (Imperative)	Whether or not		
팔지 마세요	파는지	팔았는지	팔지
palji maseyo	paneunji	paranneunji	palji

(tell someone) that / (tell someone) to

(tell someone) that	(tell someone) to
판다고	팔라고
pandago	pallago

Sample Sentences

1. 그 카메라 아직 팔지 마세요.
   Please don't sell that camera yet.

2. 거실에 있는 피아노 판다고 하지 않았어요?
   Didn't you say you were going to sell that piano in the living room?

3. 얼마에 팔지 아직 고민 중이에요.
   I'm still not sure how much I am going to sell it for.

4. 그거 작년에 얼마에 팔았는지 알아요?
   Do you know how much they sold that for last year?

5. 그거 저한테 파세요.
   Please sell that to me.

Quiz

1. 그 피아노 절대 (   ).
   Please don't ever sell that piano.

2. 엄마가 집에 있는 도자기 (   ) 하셨어요.
   My mom said she's going to sell the china in our house.

3. 언제 (   ) 아직 안 정했어요.
   I haven't decided when I'm going to sell it.

누구 기다려요?

Who are you waiting for?

기다리다
to wait

Conjugation

기다리다
gi-da-ri-da

Present	Past	Future / Guessing	Present Progressive
기다려요	기다렸어요	기다릴 거예요	기다리고 있어요
gidaryeoyo	gidaryeosseoyo	gidaril geoyeyo	gidarigo isseoyo

Imperative

기다리세요	기다려요	기다려	기다려라
gidariseyo	gidaryeoyo	gidaryeo	gidaryeora

Modifier

기다린	기다리는	기다릴	기다리던	기다렸던
gidarin	gidarineun	gidaril	gidarideon	gidaryeotteon

Want	Can
기다리고 싶어요	기다릴 수 있어요
gidarigo sipeoyo	gidaril su isseoyo

Don't (Imperative)	Whether or not		
기다리지 마세요	기다리는지	기다렸는지	기다릴지
gidariji maseyo	gidarineunji	gidaryeonneunji	gidarilji

(tell someone) that	(tell someone) to
기다린다고	기다리라고
gidarindago	gidarirago

Sample Sentences

Track 46

1. 드디어 기다리던 앨범이 나왔어요.
   The album I've been waiting for has finally come out.

2. 저 기다릴 수 있어요?
   Can you wait for me?

3. 저 많이 늦을 것 같으니까 기다리지 마세요.
   I think I'm going to be really late, so please don't wait up.

4. 삼십 분째 현우 씨를 기다리고 있어요.
   I have been waiting for Hyunwoo for 30 minutes now.

5. 오래 기다렸어요?
   Did you wait for a long time?

Quiz

1. 혼자서 (   )?
   Can you wait by yourself?

2. 오늘 집에 안 돌아오니까 (   ).
   I'm not coming back home today, so please don't wait up.

3. 밖에서 (   )?
   Did you wait outside?

Answers :
1. 기다릴 수 있어요 / 2. 기다리지 마세요 / 3. 기다렸어요

171

달리다
to run

Conjugation

달리다
dal-li-da

Present	Past	Future / Guessing	Present Progressive
달려요	달렸어요	달릴 거예요	달리고 있어요
dallyeoyo	dallyeosseoyo	dallil geoyeyo	dalligo isseoyo

Imperative

달리세요	달려요	달려	달려라
dalliseyo	dallyeoyo	dallyeo	dallyeora

Modifier

달린	달리는	달릴	달리던	달렸던
dallin	dallineun	dallil	dallideon	dallyeotteon

Want / Can

Want	Can
달리고 싶어요	달릴 수 있어요
dalligo sipeoyo	dallil su isseoyo

Don't (Imperative) / Whether or not

Don't (Imperative)	Whether or not		
달리지 마세요	달리는지	달렸는지	달릴지
dalliji maseyo	dallineunji	dallyeonneunji	dallilji

(tell someone) that / (tell someone) to

(tell someone) that	(tell someone) to
달린다고	달리라고
dallindago	dallirago

Sample Sentences

1. 오늘 아침에 운동장에서 달렸어요.
   I also ran on a school playground today in the morning.

2. 너무 빨리 달리지 마세요.
   Please don't run too fast.

3. 얼마나 빨리 달릴 수 있어요?
   How fast can you run?

4. 늦었으면 빨리 달리세요.
   If you are late, please run fast.

5. 하이힐을 신고 어떻게 달려요?
   How can you run in high heels?

Quiz

1. 어제 운동하려고 공원에서 (   ).
   I ran in a park for exercise yesterday.

2. 복도에서 (   ).
   Please don't run in the hallway.

3. 이기고 싶으면 빨리 (   ).
   If you want to win, please run fast.

Answers :
1. 달렸어요 / 2. 달리지 마세요 / 3. 달리세요 or 달려요

읽다
to read

Conjugation

Present	Past	Future / Guessing	Present Progressive
읽어요	읽었어요	읽을 거예요	읽고 있어요
ilgeoyo	ilgeosseoyo	ilgeul geoyeyo	ilkko isseoyo

Imperative

읽으세요	읽어요	읽어	읽어라
ilgeuseyo	ilgeoyo	ilgeo	ilgeora

Modifier

읽은	읽는	읽을	읽던	읽었던
ilgeun	ingneun	ilgeul	ilkdeon	ilgeotteon

Want / Can

Want	Can
읽고 싶어요	읽을 수 있어요
ilkko sipeoyo	ilgeul su isseoyo

Don't (Imperative) / Whether or not

Don't (Imperative)	Whether or not		
읽지 마세요	읽는지	읽었는지	읽을지
ilkji maseyo	ingneunji	ilgeonneunji	ilgeulji

(tell someone) that / (tell someone) to

(tell someone) that	(tell someone) to
읽는다고	읽으라고
ingneundago	ilgeurago

Sample Sentences

1. 큰 소리로 읽으세요
   Please read it out loud.

2. 오늘 신문 읽었어요?
   Did you read the newspaper today?

3. 어두운 곳에서 책 읽지 마세요.
   Please don't read books in dark places.

4. 저는 소설책만 읽어요.
   I only read novels.

5. 시험 끝나면 책 많이 읽을 거예요.
   After I finish my exams, I'm going to read a lot of books.

Quiz

1. 제가 빌려준 책 (   )?
   Did you read the book I lent you?

2. 오스카 씨는 이 작가 책만 (   ).
   Oscar only reads this author's books.

3. 휴가 때 부모님 집에 가면 만화책 많이 (   ).
   When I go to my parents' house during the holiday, I'm going to read a lot of comic books.

Answers :
1. 읽었어요 / 2. 읽어요 / 3. 읽을 거예요

177

쓰다

to write

The Korean Verbs Guide - Vol.1

Conjugation

쓰다
sseu-da

Present	Past	Future / Guessing	Present Progressive
써요 sseoyo	썼어요 sseosseoyo	쓸 거예요 sseul geoyeyo	쓰고 있어요 sseugo isseoyo

Imperative

쓰세요 sseuseyo	써요 sseoyo	써 sseo	써라 sseora

Modifier

쓴 sseun	쓰는 sseuneun	쓸 sseul	쓰던 sseudeon	썼던 sseotteon

Want	Can
쓰고 싶어요 sseugo sipeoyo	쓸 수 있어요 sseul su isseoyo

Don't (Imperative)	Whether or not		
쓰지 마세요 sseuji maseyo	쓰는지 sseuneunji	썼는지 sseonneunji	쓸지 sseulji

(tell someone) that	(tell someone) to
쓴다고 sseundago	쓰라고 sseurago

Sample Sentences

1. 한국어로 일기 쓰고 싶어요.
   I want to write a diary in Korean.

2. 그 책 쓴 작가가 누구죠?
   Who is the author who wrote that book?

3. 어디에 썼는지 잊어버렸어요.
   I don't remember where I wrote it.

4. 지금 보고서 쓰고 있어요.
   I am writing a report right now.

5. 제 이름 한자로 쓸 수 있어요.
   I can write my name in Chinese characters.

Quiz

1. 이 책 (　　) 작가 이름 알아요?
   Do you know the name of the author who wrote this book?

2. 누가 (　　　　) 알아요.
   I know who wrote it.

3. 한국어로 '안녕하세요' (　　　　　　).
   I can write 'hello' in Korean.

Answers :
1. 쓴 / 2. 썼는지 / 3. 쓸 수 있어요

The Korean Verbs Guide - Vol.1

무섭다

to be scary; to be scared, to be afraid of

Conjugation

무섭다
mu-seop-da

Present	Past	Future / Guessing	Present Progressive
무서워요 museowoyo	무서웠어요 museowosseoyo	무서울 거예요 museo-ul geoyeyo	–

Imperative

–	–	–	–

Modifier

무서운 museo-un	–	무서울 museo-ul	무섭던 museopdeon	무서웠던 museowotteon

Want		Can	
–		무서울 수 있어요 museo-ul su isseoyo	

Don't (Imperative)	Whether or not		
–	무서운지 museo-unji	무서웠는지 museowonneunji	무서울지 museo-ulji

(tell someone) that	(tell someone) to
무섭다고 museopdago	–

The Korean Verbs Guide - Vol.1

Sample Sentences

1. 무서운 얘기 해 주세요.
   Please tell me a scary story.

2. 소문이란 게 얼마나 무서운지 알게 됐어요.
   I learned just how scary rumors are.

3. 추리 소설을 밤에 읽으면 진짜 무서워요.
   It is really scary if you read detective stories at night.

4. 뭐가 무서운지 말해 보세요.
   Please tell me what is scary.

5. 효진 씨가 무섭다고 저한테 같이 가자고 했어요.
   Hyojin said she was too scared (to go by herself), so she asked me to go with her.

Quiz

1. 밤에 혼자 자는 게 얼마나 (   ) 알아요?
   Do you know how scary sleeping alone at night is?

2. 공포 영화를 혼자 보면 정말 (   ).
   It is scary if you watch a horror movie alone.

3. 은수 씨가 (   ) 전화했어요.
   Eunsu called me saying she was scared.

Answers :
1. 무서운지 / 2. 무섭습니다 / 3. 무섭다고

183

About the Photographs Used in This Book

The photographs in this book were taken and provided by Ryan Cabal, an avid Talk To Me In Korean listener and photographer from the U.S., who lived in Seoul for many years. For inquiries regarding any of the photos used in this book, please contact the Talk To Me In Korean team at contact@talktomeinkorean.com.

THE KOREAN VERBS GUIDE
Vol. 2

written and designed by
Talk To Me In Korean

The **Korean Verbs** Guide Vol.2
한국어 학습자가 반드시 알아야 할 **동사 가이드**

1판 1쇄 · 1st edition published	2013. 12. 2.
개정판 1쇄 · 1st revised edition published	2025. 4. 7.

지은이 · Written by	Talk To Me In Korean
책임편집 · Edited by	안효진 Hyojin Ahn, 스테파니 베이츠 Stephanie Bates
디자인 · Designed by	선윤아 Yoona Sun
일러스트 · Illustrations by	장성원 Sungwon Jang
사진 · Photographs by	라이언 카발 Ryan Cabal
녹음 · Voice Recordings by	안효진 Hyojin Ahn
펴낸곳 · Published by	롱테일북스 Longtail Books
펴낸이 · Publisher	이수영 Suyoung Lee
편집 · Copy-edited by	김보경 Florence Kim
주소 · Address	04033 서울특별시 마포구 양화로 113, 3층(서교동, 순흥빌딩)
	3rd Floor, 113 Yanghwa-ro, Mapo-gu, Seoul, KOREA
이메일 · E-mail	editor@ltinc.net
ISBN	978-1-942791-60-7 13710

TTMIK - TALK TO ME IN KOREAN

THE KOREAN VERBS GUIDE

Vol.2

한국어 학습자가 반드시 알아야 할
동사 가이드

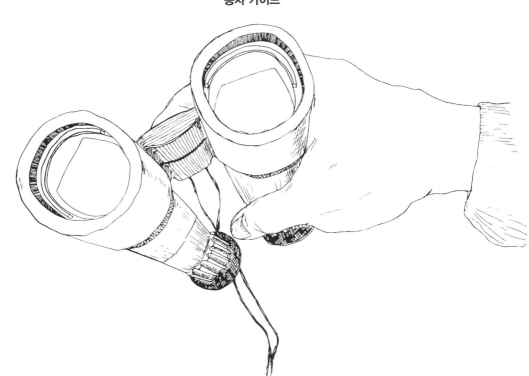

Index for Volume 1

How To Use This Book 6

General Rules of Verb Conjugation in Korean 8

Index for Volume 2

만나다
to meet (up)

Conjugation

만나다
man-na-da

Present	Past	Future / Guessing	Present Progressive
만나요	만났어요	만날 거예요	만나고 있어요
mannayo	mannasseoyo	mannal geoyeyo	mannago isseoyo

Imperative

만나세요	만나요	만나	만나라
mannaseyo	mannayo	manna	mannara

Modifier

만난	만나는	만날	만나던	만났던
mannan	mannaneun	mannal	mannadeon	mannattteon

Want	Can
만나고 싶어요	만날 수 있어요
mannago sipeoyo	mannal su isseoyo

Don't (Imperative)	Whether or not		
만나지 마세요	만나는지	만났는지	만날지
mannaji maseyo	mannaneunji	mannanneunji	mannaljji

(tell someone) that	(tell someone) to
만난다고	만나라고
mannandago	manarago

Sample Sentences

1. 내일 석진 씨 만날 거예요.
   I'm going to meet Seokjin tomorrow.

2. 아직 몇 시에 만날지 안 정했어요.
   We haven't decided what time we are going to meet yet.

3. 다음주에 누구 만난다고 했죠?
   Who did you say you were going to meet next week?

4. 지금 친구 만나고 있어요.
   I am with my friends right now.

5. 우리 언제 처음 만났는지 기억해요?
   Do you remember when we first met?

Quiz

1. 다음주에 홍대에서 민정 씨 (   ).
   I'm going to meet Minjeong next week in Hongdae.

2. 파리에서 클라라 씨 언제 (   ) 했죠?
   When did you say you were going to meet Clara in Paris?

3. 우리 내일 언제 (   ) 정해요.
   Let's decide when we will meet tomorrow.

Answers :
1. 만날 거예요 / 2. 만난다고 / 3. 만날지

The Korean Verbs Guide - vol.2

얻다

to get, to acquire,
to gain

Conjugation

얻다
eot-da

Present	Past	Future / Guessing	Present Progressive
얻어요	얻었어요	얻을 거예요	얻고 있어요
eodeoyo	eodeosseoyo	eodeul geoyeyo	eotgo isseoyo

Imperative

얻으세요	얻어요	얻어	얻어라
eodeuseyo	eodeoyo	eodeo	eodeora

Modifier

얻은	얻는	얻을	얻던	얻었던
eodeun	eonneun	eodeul	eottteon	eodeottteon

Want	Can
얻고 싶어요	얻을 수 있어요
eotkko sipeoyo	eodeul su isseoyo

Don't (Imperative)	Whether or not		
얻지 마세요	얻는지	얻었는지	얻을지
eotjji maseyo	eonneunji	eodeonneunji	eodeuljji

(tell someone) that	(tell someone) to
얻는다고	얻으라고
eonneundago	eodeurago

Sample Sentences

1. 지난번 일을 계기로 자신감을 많이 얻었어요.
   I gained a lot of confidence after finishing the last task.

2. 제가 인터넷에서 얻은 정보가 잘못된 정보인가 봐요.
   It seems that the information I got from the Internet was wrong.

3. 방 세 개짜리 집을 얻고 싶어요.
   I want to get a house with three rooms.

4. 여기서 많은 정보를 얻을 수 있어요.
   You can find a lot of information here.

5. 그 회사 홈페이지에 가면 많은 정보를 얻을 수 있어요.
   If you go to that company's homepage, you can find a lot of information.

Quiz

1. 어제 있었던 일로 자신감을 조금 (   ).
   I gained a little bit of confidence after what happened yesterday.

2. 어제 지영 씨한테 (   ) 정보가 잘못된 정보였어요.
   The information I got from Jiyoung yesterday was wrong.

3. 거기서도 여행에 관련된 정보를 (   )?
   Can you find information about traveling there too?

Answers :
1. 얻었어요 / 2. 얻은 / 3. 얻을 수 있어요

13

혼자서도 10분 안에
만들 수 있어요.

I can even make it by myself in ten minutes.

만들다
to make

Conjugation

Present	Past	Future / Guessing	Present Progressive
만들어요	만들었어요	만들 거예요	만들고 있어요
mandeureoyo	mandeureosseoyo	mandeul geoyeyo	mandeulgo isseoyo

Imperative

만드세요	만들어요	만들어	만들어라
mandeuseyo	mandeureoyo	mandeureo	mandeureora

Modifier

만든	만드는	만들	만들던	만들었던
mandeun	mandeuneun	mandeul	mandeuldeon	mandeureottteon

Want

만들고 싶어요	
mandeulgo sipeoyo	

Can

	만들 수 있어요
	mandeul su isseoyo

Don't (Imperative)

만들지 마세요	만드는지	만들었는지	만들지
mandeulji maseyo	mandeuneunji	mandeureonneunji	mandeuljji

Whether or not

(tell someone) that

만든다고	
mandeundago	

(tell someone) to

	만들라고
	mandeullago

Sample Sentences

1. 이거 친구 주려고 만들었어요.
   I made this to give to my friend.

2. 제가 만든 떡볶이가 맛이 없어요?
   Was the tteokbokki I made not delicious?

3. 재밌는 영상을 만들고 싶어요.
   I want to make funny videos.

4. 어떻게 만드는지 모르겠어요.
   I don't know how to make it.

5. 혼자서도 10분 안에 만들 수 있어요.
   I can even make it by myself in ten minutes.

Quiz

1. 제 친구가 (   ) 김밥 맛있어요?
   Did the Gimbap my friend made taste delicious?

2. 좋은 노래를 (   ).
   I want to make good songs.

3. 어디서 (   ) 아세요?
   Do you know where they make it?

Answers :
1. 만든 / 2. 만들고 싶어요 / 3. 만드는지

17

잃어버리다

to lose (something)

Conjugation

잃어버리다
i-reo-beo-ri-da

Present	Past	Future / Guessing	Present Progressive
잃어버려요	잃어버렸어요	잃어버릴 거예요	–
ireobeoryeoyo	ireobeoryeosseoyo	irreobeoril geoyeyo	

Imperative

– – – –

Modifier

잃어버린	잃어버리는	잃어버릴	잃어버리던	잃어버렸던
ireobeorin	ireobeorineun	ireobeoril	ireobeorideon	ireobeoryeottteon

Want

–

Can

잃어버릴 수 있어요
ireobeoril su isseoyo

Don't (Imperative)

잃어버리지 마세요
ireobeoriji maseyo

Whether or not

잃어버리는지	잃어버렸는지	잃어버릴지
ireobeorineunji	ireobeoryeonneunji	ireobeoriljji

(tell someone) that

잃어버린다고
ireobeorindago

(tell someone) to

–

Sample Sentences

1. 저는 물건을 잘 잃어버려요.
   I lose things often.

2. 중요한 거니까 잃어버리지 마세요.
   This is really important, so don't lose it.

3. 어디서 잃어버렸는지 알아요?
   Do you know where you lost it?

4. 잃어버린 장갑 찾았어요?
   Did you find the gloves you lost?

5. 작년에 잃어버렸던 책을 침대 밑에서 찾았어요.
   I found the book that I lost last year under my bed.

Quiz

1. 저는 평소에 물건 잘 안 (   ).
   I don't usually lose things.

2. 비싼거니까 절대로 (   ).
   It's expensive, so don't ever lose it, please.

3. 언제 (   ) 기억나요?
   Do you remember when you lost it?

Answers :
1. 잃어버려요 / 2. 잃어버리지 마세요 / 3. 잃어버렸는지

잊어버리다
to forget

Conjugation

잊어버리다
i-jeo-beo-ri-da

Present	Past	Future / Guessing	Present Progressive
잊어버려요 ijeobeoryeoyo	잊어버렸어요 ijeobeoryeosseoyo	잊어버릴 거예요 ijeobeoril geoyeyo	–

Imperative

잊어버리세요 ijeobeoriseyo	잊어버려요 ijeobeoryeoyo	잊어버려 ijeobeoryeo	잊어버려라 ijeobeoryeora

Modifier

잊어버린 ijeobeorin	잊어버리는 ijeobeorineun	잊어버릴 ijeobeoril	잊어버리던 ijeobeorideon	잊어버렸던 ijeobeoryeottteon

Want	Can
잊어버리고 싶어요 ijeobeorigo sipeoyo	잊어버릴 수 있어요 ijeobeoril su isseoyo

Don't (Imperative)	Whether or not		
잊어버리지 마세요 ijeobeoriji maseyo	잊어버리는지 ijeobeorineunji	잊어버렸는지 ijeobeoryeonneunji	잊어버릴지 ijeobeoriljji

(tell someone) that	(tell someone) to
잊어버린다고 ijeobeorindago	잊어버리라고 ijeobeorirago

Sample Sentences

1. 수영 씨 결혼식이 언제인지 잊어버렸어요.
   I forgot when Sooyoung's wedding is.

2. 그냥 잊어버리세요.
   Just forget it.

3. 어차피 시험 끝나면 오늘 외운 거 다 잊어버릴 거예요.
   Regardless, I am going to forget all of the things I memorized today once the exam is over.

4. 저는 사람들 이름을 자꾸 잊어버려요.
   I forget people's names a lot.

5. 친구가 지갑을 잃어버려서 속상해하길래 그냥 잊어버리라고 했어요.
   My friend was upset because he lost his wallet, so I just told him to forget about it.

Quiz

1. 재석 씨 연주회가 몇 시인지 (   ).
   I forgot what time Jaeseok's recital is.

2. 제 친구는 중요한 일은 다 (   ).
   A friend of mine forgets all important things.

3. 친구가 좋아하는 여자한테 고백했다가 거절당해서 슬퍼하길래 그냥
   (   ) 했어요.
   My friend was upset because he was rejected by the girl he likes when he confessed to her, so I just told him to forget about her.

Answers :
1. 잊어버렸어요 / 2. 잊어버려요 / 3. 잊어버리라고

23

좋다

to be good;
to like

The Korean Verbs Guide - vol.2

Conjugation

좋다
jo-ta

Present	Past	Future / Guessing	Present Progressive
좋아요	좋았어요	좋을 거예요	–
joayo	joasseoyo	joeul geoyeyo	

Imperative

–	–	–	–

Modifier

좋은	–	좋을	좋던	좋았던
joeun		jo-eul	joteon	joattteon

Want	Can
–	좋을 수 있어요
	jo-eul su isseoyo

Don't (Imperative)	Whether or not		
–	좋은지	좋았는지	좋을지
	jo-eunji	joanneunji	joeuljji

(tell someone) that	(tell someone) to
좋다고	–
jotago	

Sample Sentences

1. 뭐가 좋은지 저도 모르겠어요.
   I don't know which one is good, either.

2. 지나고 나니까 좋았던 기억밖에 없어요.
   Now that it's over, I only have good memories left.

3. 언제가 좋을지 말해 주세요.
   Let me know when would be a good time for you.

4. 선생님이 좋다고 하셨어요.
   My teacher said it was good.

5. 사람이 많으면 많을수록 좋아요.
   The more people, the better.

Quiz

1. 지금 생각해보면 (   ) 기억이 나빴던 기억보다 더 많아요.
   Now that I look back, I have more good memories left than bad memories.

2. 누가 이 역할을 맡으면 (   ) 추천해 주세요.
   Please recommend (someone) who would be good to take on this role.

3. 패스트푸드는 적게 먹으면 먹을수록 (   ).
   The less junk food you eat, the better.

Answers :
1. 좋았던 / 2. 좋을지 / 3. 좋아요

좋아하다
to like

Conjugation

좋아하다
jo-a-ha-da

Present	Past	Future / Guessing	Present Progressive
좋아해요	좋아했어요	좋아할 거예요	좋아하고 있어요
joahaeyo	joahaesseoyo	joahal geoyeyo	joahago isseoyo

Imperative

–	–	–	–

Modifier

좋아한	좋아하는	좋아할	좋아하던	좋아했던
joahan	joahaneun	joahal	joahadeon	joahaettteon

Want	Can
좋아하고 싶어요	좋아할 수 있어요
joahago sipeoyo	joahal su isseoyo

Don't (Imperative)	Whether or not		
좋아하지 마세요	좋아하는지	좋아했는지	좋아할지
joahaji maseyo	joahaneunji	joahaenneunji	joahaljji

(tell someone) that	(tell someone) to
좋아한다고	좋아하라고
joahandago	joaharago

Sample Sentences

1. 제가 뭘 좋아하는지 아직도 몰라요?
   You still don't know what I like?

2. 제일 좋아하는 운동이 뭐예요?
   What is your favorite sport?

3. 와인 좋아해요?
   Do you like wine?

4. 공짜 너무 좋아하지 마세요.
   Don't like free things too much.

5. 이 선물을 받으면 친구가 정말 좋아할 거예요.
   My friend would really like it if she got this as a present.

Quiz

1. 경화 씨가 꽃 (   ) 몰랐어요.
   I didn't know Kyung-hwa likes flowers.

2. 요즘 제일 (   ) 드라마가 뭐예요?
   What drama do you like the best these days?

3. 강아지 (   )?
   Do you like puppies?

Answers :
1. 좋아하는지 / 2. 좋아하는 / 3. 좋아해요

29

이 분이 마시는 커피랑 똑같은 걸로 주세요.

Please give me the same coffee this person is drinking.

마시다
to drink

Conjugation

마시다
ma-si-da

Present	Past	Future / Guessing	Present Progressive
마셔요 masyeoyo	마셨어요 masyeosseoyo	마실 거예요 masil geoyeyo	마시고 있어요 masigo isseoyo

Imperative

드세요 deuseyo	마셔요 masyeoyo	마셔 masyeo	마셔라 masyeora

Modifier

마신 masin	마시는 masineun	마실 masil	마시던 masideon	마셨던 masyeottteon

Want / Can

Want	Can
마시고 싶어요 masigo sipeoyo	마실 수 있어요 masil su isseoyo

Don't (Imperative) / Whether or not

Don't (Imperative)	Whether or not		
마시지 마세요 masiji maseyo	마시는지 masineunji	마셨는지 masyeonneunji	마실지 masiljji

(tell someone) that / (tell someone) to

(tell someone) that	(tell someone) to
마신다고 masindago	마시라고 masirago

Sample Sentences

1. 이 분이 마시는 커피랑 똑같은 걸로 주세요.
   Please give me the same coffee this person is drinking.

2. 물 마시고 싶어요.
   I want to drink water.

3. 커피 누구랑 마셨어요?
   With whom did you drink coffee?

4. 이 물은 더러우니까 마시지 마세요.
   This water is dirty, so please don't drink it.

5. 우유를 따뜻하게 데워서 마실 거예요.
   I will drink the milk after heating it up.

Quiz

1. 저 사람이 (   ) 주스랑 똑같은 걸로 주세요.
   Please give me the same juice that person is drinking.

2. 스무디 (   ).
   I want to drink a smoothie.

3. 이 음료수 (   ). 맛이 이상해요.
   Please don't drink this beverage. It tastes weird.

Answers :
1. 마시는 / 2. 마시고 싶어요 / 3. 마시지 마세요

33

정하다
to decide

Conjugation

정하다
jeong-ha-da

Present	*Past*	*Future / Guessing*	*Present Progressive*
정해요	정했어요	정할 거예요	정하고 있어요
jeong-haeyo	jeong-haesseoyo	jeong-hal geoyeyo	jeong-hago isseoyo

Imperative

정하세요	정해요	정해	정해라
jeong-haseyo	jeong-haeyo	jeong-hae	jeong-haera

Modifier

정한	정하는	정할	정하던	정했던
jeong-han	jeong-haneun	jeong-hal	jeong-hadeon	jeong-haettteon

Want	*Can*
정하고 싶어요	정할 수 있어요
jeong-hago sipeopyo	jeong-hal su isseoyo

Don't (Imperative)	*Whether or not*		
정하지 마세요	정하는지	정했는지	정할지
jeong-haji maseyo	jeong-haneunji	jeong-haenneunji	jeong-haljji

(tell someone) that	*(tell someone) to*
정한다고	정하라고
jeong-handago	jeong-harago

Sample Sentences

1. 저녁 뭐 먹을지 정했어요?
   Did you decide what you are going to eat for dinner?

2. 혼자서 정하지 마세요.
   Don't decide by yourself.

3. 장소랑 시간은 스테파니 씨가 정한다고 했어요.
   Stephanie will decide the time and date.

4. 지금 당장 정하라고 하면 전 어떡해요?
   If you tell me to decide right away, what am I supposed to do?

5. 이렇게 정한 이유가 있어요?
   Is there a reason why you decided (to do it) like this?

Quiz

1. 이따가 뭐 할지 (   )?
   Did you decide what you are going to do later today?

2. 지금은 아무것도 (   ).
   Don't decide anything for now, please.

3. 이 많은 걸 저 혼자 (   ) 하면 전 어떡해요?
   If you tell me to decide this many things, what am I supposed to do?

Answers :
1. 정했어요 / 2. 정하지 마세요 / 3. 정하라고

The Korean Verbs Guide - vol.2

바꾸다

to change

Conjugation

바꾸다
ba-kku-da

Present	Past	Future / Guessing	Present Progressive
바꿔요	바꿨어요	바꿀 거예요	바꾸고 있어요
bakkwoyo	bakkwosseoyo	bakkul geoyeyo	bakkugo isseoyo

Imperative

바꾸세요	바꿔요	바꿔	바꿔라
bakkuseyo	bakkwoyo	bakkwo	bakkwora

Modifier

바꾼	바꾸는	바꿀	바꾸던	바꿨던
bakkun	bakkuneun	bakkul	bakkudeon	bakkwotteon

Want | Can

Want	Can
바꾸고 싶어요	바꿀 수 있어요
bakkugo sipeoyo	bakkul su isseoyo

Don't (Imperative) | Whether or not

Don't (Imperative)	Whether or not		
바꾸지 마세요	바꾸는지	바꿨는지	바꿀지
bakkuji maseyo	bakkuneunji	bakkwonneunji	bakkuljji

(tell someone) that | (tell someone) to

(tell someone) that	(tell someone) to
바꾼다고	바꾸라고
bakkundago	bakkurago

Sample Sentences

1. 저 이름 바꿀 거예요.
   I am going to change my name.

2. 보고서 주제를 어제 바꿨어요.
   I changed the topic for my report yesterday.

3. 전화번호를 바꿨는지 몰랐어요.
   I didn't know you changed your phone number.

4. 지금 당장 일정을 바꾸라고 하세요.
   Please tell them to change the schedule immediately.

5. 핸드폰을 최신 모델로 바꾸고 싶어요.
   I want to change my phone to the newest model, too.

Quiz

1. 수미 씨 이름 (   ) 알았어요?
   You knew Soomi changed her name?

2. 전화로 계획을 (   ) 하세요.
   Please tell them to change the plan via phone.

3. 컴퓨터를 새 걸로 (   ) 싶어요.
   I want to change my computer to a new one.

Answers :
1. 바꿨는지 / 2. 바꾸라고 / 3. 바꾸고

39

알다

to know

Conjugation

알다
al-da

Present	*Past*	*Future / Guessing*	*Present Progressive*
알아요	알았어요	알 거예요	알고 있어요
arayo	arasseoyo	al geoyeyo	algo isseoyo

Imperative

—   —   —   —

Modifier

안	아는	알	알던	알았던
an	aneun	al	aldeon	arattteon

Want	*Can*
알고 싶어요	알 수 있어요
algo sipeoyo	al su isseoyo

Don't (Imperative)	*Whether or not*		
—	아는지	알았는지	알지
	aneunji	aranneunji	aljji

(tell someone) that	*(tell someone) to*
안다고	알라고
andago	allago

Sample Sentences

1. 이 문제의 정답을 아는 사람이 아무도 없어요?
   Is there no one who knows the answer to this question?

2. 제가 아는 사람하고 닮았어요.
   You look like someone I know.

3. 이 책을 보면 알 수 있어요.
   You will know if you look at this book.

4. 뭘 그렇게 알고 싶어요?
   What do you want to know so badly?

5. 준영 씨가 아는지 모르는지 모르겠어요.
   I don't know if Jun-yeong knows or not.

Quiz

1. 제가 한 질문의 정답을 (   ) 사람은 손 드세요.
   Anyone who knows the answer to the question I asked, please raise
   your hand.

2. 선생님께 여쭤보면 (   ).
   If you ask your teacher, you will find out.

3. 수아 씨가 (   ) 모르는지 물어보세요.
   Please ask if Su-ah knows or not.

Answers :
1. 아는 / 2. 알 수 있어요 / 3. 아는지

버스 안이 정말 좁아요.

The inside of the bus is really narrow.

좀다
to be narrow,
to be small (space)

Conjugation

좁다
jop-tta

Present	Past	Future / Guessing	Present Progressive
좁아요	좁았어요	좁을 거예요	–
jobayo	jobasseoyo	jobeul geoyeyo	

Imperative

–	–	–	–

Modifier

좁은	–	좁을	좁던	좁았던
jobeun		jobeul	joptteon	jobattteon

Want	Can
–	좁을 수 있어요
	jobeul su isseoyo

Don't (Imperative)	Whether or not		
–	좁은지	좁았는지	좁을지
	jobeunji	jobanneunji	jobeuljji

(tell someone) that	(tell someone) to
좁다고	좁으라고
jopttago	jobeurago

Sample Sentences

1. 이렇게 좁은 방에 사람이 15명이나 들어올 수 있다고요?
   Are you saying that 15 people can come in a small room like this?

2. 얼마나 좁은지 물어봐 주세요.
   Please ask how small it is.

3. 열 명이 들어가면 좁을 거예요.
   If ten people go in, it will be small.

4. 저는 넓은 집보다 좁은 집이 좋아요.
   I like small houses more than wide houses.

5. 세상 참 좁아요.
   The world is really small. (What a small world.)

Quiz

1. 그렇게 (   ) 소파 위에서 잠을 자겠다고요?
   Are you saying that you are going to sleep on a small couch like that?

2. 얼마나 (   ) 눈으로 직접 확인해 주세요.
   Please check with your own eyes how small it is.

3. 거기 다섯 명이 다 앉으면 (   ).
   If all five people sit on there, it will be small.

Answers :
1. 좁은 / 2. 좁은지 / 3. 좁을 거예요.

넓다

to be wide,
to be big (space)

Conjugation

넓다
neol-tta

Present	Past	Future / Guessing	Present Progressive
넓어요 neolbeoyo	넓었어요 neolbeosseoyo	넓을 거예요 neolbeul geoyeyo	–

Imperative

–	–	–	–

Modifier

넓은 neolbeun	–	넓을 neolbeul	넓던 neoltteon	넓었던 neolbeottteon

Want	Can
–	넓을 수 있어요 neolbeul su isseoyo

Don't (Imperative)	Whether or not		
–	넓은지 neolbeunji	넓었는지 neolbeonneunji	넓을지 neolbeuljji

(tell someone) that	(tell someone) to
넓다고 neolttago	넓으라고 neolbeurago

Sample Sentences

1. 현우 씨는 그 방이 너무 넓다고 싫대요.
   Hyunwoo said he didn't like the room because it's too wide.

2. 저는 넓은 방이 좋아요.
   I like big rooms.

3. 방이 굉장히 넓어요.
   The room is very wide.

4. 얼마나 넓은지 물어봤어요?
   Did you ask them how wide it is?

5. 이번에 이사가는 집은 얼마나 넓어요?
   How big is the house you are moving to?

Quiz

1. 수지 씨는 TV 화면 너무 (   ) 싫대요.
   Suji said she didn't like the TV screen because it's too wide.

2. 중기 씨는 (   ) 도로가 좋대요.
   Joong-ki said he likes wide roads.

3. 어제 산 핸드폰은 화면이 얼마나 (   )?
   How big is the screen of the phone you bought yesterday?

Answers :
1. 넓다고 / 2. 넓은 / 3. 넓어요

떠나다
to leave

Conjugation

떠나다
tteo-na-da

Present	Past	Future / Guessing	Present Progressive
떠나요	떠났어요	떠날 거예요	떠나고 있어요
tteonayo	tteonasseoyo	tteonal geoyeyo	tteonago isseoyo

Imperative

떠나세요	떠나요	떠나	떠나라
tteonaseyo	tteonayo	tteona	tteonara

Modifier

떠난	떠나는	떠날	떠나던	떠났던
tteonan	tteonaneun	tteonal	tteonadeon	tteonattteon

Want	Can
떠나고 싶어요	떠날 수 있어요
tteonago sipeyo	tteonal su isseoyo

Don't (Imperative)	Whether or not		
떠나지 마세요	떠나는지	떠났는지	떠날지
tteonaji maseyo	tteonaneunji	tteonanneunji	tteonalji

(tell someone) that	(tell someone) to
떠난다고	떠나라고
tteonandago	tteonarago

Sample Sentences

1. 지금 당장 떠나세요.
   Please leave right now.

2. 이제 떠날 시간이에요.
   It is time to leave now.

3. 지금 당장 떠날 수 있어요.
   I can leave right now.

4. 미영 씨가 언제 떠났는지 알아요?
   Do you know when Miyeong left?

5. 저 혼자 두고 떠나지 마세요.
   Please don't leave me by myself and go (alone).

Quiz

1. 엄마가 오시면 같이 (   ).
   When your mom comes, leave with her, please.

2. 저는 언제든지 (   ).
   I can leave any time.

3. 아직 (   ).
   Please don't leave yet.

Answers :
1. 떠나세요 or 떠나요 / 2. 떠날 수 있어요 / 3. 떠나지 마세요

The Korean Verbs Guide - vol.2

때리다

to hit (someone)

Conjugation

때리다
ttae-ri-da

Present	Past	Future / Guessing	Present Progressive
때려요 ttaeryeoyo	때렸어요 ttaeryeosseoyo	때릴 거예요 ttaeril geoyeyo	때리고 있어요 ttaerigo isseoyo

Imperative

때리세요 ttaeriseyo	때려요 ttaeryeoyo	때려 ttaeryeo	때려라 ttaeryeora

Modifier

때린 ttaerin	때리는 ttaerineun	때릴 ttaeril	때리던 ttaerideon	때렸던 ttaeryeottteon

Want	Can
때리고 싶어요 ttaerigo sipeoyo	때릴 수 있어요 ttaeril su isseoyo

Don't (Imperative)	Whether or not		
때리지 마세요 ttaeriji maseyo	때리는지 ttaerineunji	때렸는지 ttaeryeonneunji	때릴지 ttaeriljji

(tell someone) that	(tell someone) to
때린다고 ttaerindago	때리라고 ttaerirago

Sample Sentences

1. 자꾸 그런 말 하면 때릴 거예요.
   If you keep saying things like that, I am going to hit you.

2. 누가 때렸는지 말해 보세요.
   Please tell me who hit you.

3. 방금 나 때린 사람 나와.
   Whoever just hit me, come forward.

4. 누가 그렇게 세게 때리라고 했어요?
   Who said to hit (me) that hard?

5. 동생이 저 때렸어요.
   My little sister hit me.

Quiz

1. 자꾸 저 놀리면 진짜로 (   ).
   If you keep teasing me, I'm really going to hit you.

2. 누가 (   ) 알아요?
   Do you know who hit you?

3. 아까 제 등 (   ) 사람 누군지 알아요?
   Do you know the person who hit me in the back?

Answers :
1. 때릴 거예요 / 2. 때렸는지 / 3. 때린

55

일어나다

to wake up;
to get up

Conjugation

일어나다
i-reo-na-da

Present	Past	Future / Guessing	Present Progressive
일어나요	일어났어요	일어날 거예요	일어나고 있어요
ireonayo	ireonasseoyo	ireonal geoyeyo	ireonago isseoyo

Imperative

일어나세요	일어나요	일어나	일어나라
ireonaseyo	ireonayo	ireona	ireonara

Modifier

일어난	일어나는	일어날	일어나던	일어났던
ireonan	ireonaneun	ireonal	ireonadeon	ireonattteon

Want	*Can*
일어나고 싶어요	일어날 수 있어요
ireonago sipeoyo	ireonal su isseoyo

Don't (Imperative)	*Whether or not*		
일어나지 마세요	일어나는지	일어났는지	일어날지
ireonaji maseyo	ireonaneunji	ireonanneunji	ireonaljji

(tell someone) that	*(tell someone) to*
일어난다고	일어나라고
ireonandago	ireonarago

Sample Sentences

1. 저는 매일 아침 8시에 일어나요.
   I wake up every day at 8 in the morning.

2. 저는 아침에 일어나는 시간이 매일 달라요.
   I wake up at a different time every day.

3. 내일 몇 시에 일어날지 알려 주시면 아침 식사를 준비해 놓을게요.
   If you tell me what time you plan on waking up in the morning, I will make sure breakfast is prepared.

4. 깨워 주지 않으셔도 저 혼자 일어날 수 있어요.
   Even if you don't wake me up, I can wake up by myself.

5. 아침 일찍 일어나는 습관을 기르고 싶어요.
   I want get in the habit of waking up early in the morning.

Quiz

1. 저희 가족은 모두 매일 아침 6시에 (   ).
   Everyone in my family wakes up every day at 6 in the morning.

2. 제 동생은 주말에도 아침에 (   ) 시간이 매일 똑같아요.
   My younger sister wakes up at the same time every day, even on the weekends.

3. 알람 시계가 있어서 혼자 (   ).
   Because I have an alarmclock, I can wake up by myself.

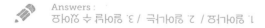

Answers :
1. 일어나요 / 2. 일어나는 / 3. 일어날 수 있어요

늦다
to be late

Conjugation

늦다
neut-tta

Present	Past	Future / Guessing	Present Progressive
늦어요	늦었어요	늦을 거예요	–
neujeoyo	neujeosseoyo	neujeul geoyeyo	

Imperative

–	–	–	–

Modifier

늦은	늦는	늦을	늦던	늦었던
neujeun	neunneun	neujeul	neuttteon	neujeottteon

Want / Can

Want	Can
–	늦을 수 있어요
	neujeul su isseoyo

Don't (Imperative) / Whether or not

Don't (Imperative)	Whether or not		
늦지 마세요	늦는지	늦었는지	늦을지
neutjji maseyo	neunneunji	neojeonneunji	neujeuljji

(tell someone) that / (tell someone) to

(tell someone) that	(tell someone) to
늦는다고	늦으라고
neunneundago	neujeurago

Sample Sentences

1. 내일은 절대 늦지 마세요.
   Please don't be late tomorrow.

2. 내일 늦는 사람은 벌금 내야 돼요.
   People who are late tomorrow have to pay a fine.

3. 지수 씨 오늘도 1시간 늦는다고 했어요.
   Jisoo said she was going to be an hour late again today.

4. 늦잠 자서 늦었어요.
   I was late because I overslept.

5. 저 오늘 좀 늦을 거예요.
   I'm going to be a little late today.

Quiz

1. 앞으로는 절대 (   ).
   From now on please don't be late.

2. 진영 씨 오늘도 (   ) 했어요?
   Did Jin-yeong say he was going to be late again today?

3. 차가 막혀서 (   ).
   I was late because there was a traffic jam.

61

제 아내는 취미로
허브를 길러요

My wife grows herbs as a hobby.

기르다

to grow; to raise

Conjugation

	Present	*Past*	*Future / Guessing*	*Present Progressive*
	길러요 gilleoyo	길렀어요 gilleosseoyo	기를 거예요 gireul geoyeyo	기르고 있어요 gireugo isseoyo

Imperative

기르세요 gireuseyo	길러요 gilleoyo	길러 gilleo	길러라 gilleora

Modifier

기른 gireun	기르는 gireuneun	기를 gireul	기르던 gireudeon	길렀던 gilleottteon

Want / *Can*

Want	*Can*
기르고 싶어요 gireugo sipeoyo	기를 수 있어요 gireul su isseoyo

Don't (Imperative) / *Whether or not*

Don't (Imperative)	*Whether or not*		
기르지 마세요 gireuji maseyo	기르는지 gireuneunji	길렀는지 gilleonneunji	기를지 gireuljji

(tell someone) that / *(tell someone) to*

(tell someone) that	*(tell someone) to*
기른다고 gireundago	기르라고 gireurago

Sample Sentences

1. 당분간 머리 안 자르고 기를 거예요.
   I'm going to stop cutting my hair for a while and just let my hair grow.

2. 이 당근을 정말 집에서 길렀어요?
   Did you really grow this carrot at home?

3. 제가 기르던 난초가 죽었어요.
   The orchids I was growing died.

4. 머리를 허리까지 기르고 싶어요.
   I want to grow my hair all the way down to my waist.

5. 제 아내는 취미로 허브를 길러요
   My wife grows herbs as a hobby.

Quiz

1. 이렇게 많은 꽃들을 혼자 (   )?
   Did you grow these many flowers all by yourself?

2. 작년부터 동생이 (   ) 선인장이 죽었어요.
   The cactus my little sister was growing died.

3. 제 친구는 집에서 방울 토마토를 (   ).
   A friend of mine grows cherry tomatoes at his house.

Answers :
1. 길렀어요 / 2. 기르던 / 3. 길러요

65

싸우다
to fight, to argue

Conjugation

싸우다
ssa-u-da

Present	Past	Future / Guessing	Present Progressive
싸워요	싸웠어요	싸울 거예요	싸우고 있어요
ssawoyo	ssawosseoyo	ssaul geoyeyo	ssaugo isseoyo

Imperative

싸우세요	싸워요	싸워	싸워라
ssauseyo	ssawoyo	ssawo	ssawora

Modifier

싸운	싸우는	싸울	싸우던	싸웠던
ssaun	ssauneun	ssaul	ssaudeon	ssawottteon

Want

싸우고 싶어요
ssaugo sipeoyo

Can

싸울 수 있어요
ssaul su isseoyo

Don't (Imperative)

싸우지 마세요
ssauji maseyo

Whether or not

싸우는지	싸웠는지	싸울지
ssauneunji	ssawonneunji	ssauljji

(tell someone) that

싸운다고
ssaundago

(tell someone) to

싸우라고
ssaurago

Sample Sentences

1. 옆 집에서 싸우는 소리가 들렸어요.
   I heard people fighting next door.

2. 그 두 사람은 자주 싸운다고 들었어요.
   I heard those two people fight a lot.

3. 밖에서 누가 지금 싸우고 있어요.
   Someone is fighting outside right now.

4. 어릴 때 저랑 자주 싸웠던 친구예요.
   He is a friend who I used to fight a lot with when we were younger.

5. 아이들끼리 놀다 보면 싸울 수 있어요.
   Sometimes kids can fight when they play with each other.

Quiz

1. 밖에서 (   ) 소리 들려요?
   Do you hear people fighting outside?

2. 지금 안에서 누가 (   )?
   Is someone fighting inside now?

3. 부부도 가끔 (   ).
   Sometimes couples can fight with each other.

Answers :
1. 싸우는 / 2. 싸우고 있어요 / 3. 싸울 수 있어요

The Korean Verbs Guide - vol.2

싸다

to be cheap,
to be inexpensive

Conjugation

싸다
ssa-da

Present		Past		Future / Guessing		Present Progressive
싸요	/	쌌어요	/	쌀 거예요	/	–
ssayo		ssasseoyo		ssal geoyeyo		

Imperative

–	/	–	/	–	/	–

Modifier

싼	/	–	/	쌀	/	싸던	/	쌌던
ssan				ssal		ssadeon		ssattteon

Want		Can
–	/	쌀 수 있어요
		ssal su isseoyo

Don't (Imperative)		Whether or not
–	/	싼지	/	쌌는지	/	쌀지
		ssanji		ssanneunji		ssaljji

(tell someone) that		(tell someone) to
싸다고	/	–
ssadago		

The Korean Verbs Guide - vol.2

Sample Sentences

Track
70

1. 그렇게 싸요?
   Is it that cheap?

2. 과일이 이렇게 쌀지 몰랐어요.
   I didn't know fruits would be so cheap here.

3. 작년에는 비쌌는데 올해는 쌀 거예요.
   It was expensive last year, but it will be cheap this year.

4. 저한테는 이게 제일 싸다고 거짓말 했어요.
   They lied and told me that this was the cheapest one.

5. 싼 볼펜을 샀더니 금방 고장 났어요.
   I bought a cheap pen and it broke quickly.

Quiz

1. 왜 그렇게 (   )?
   Why is it that cheap?

2. 그 사람이 저한테 그게 여기서 제일 (   ) 말해줬어요.
   He told me that was the cheapest here.

3. (   ) 핸드폰을 샀는데 나쁘지 않아요.
   I bought a cheap cell phone and it's not bad.

Answers :
1. 싸요 / 2. 싸다고 / 3. 싼

71

비싸다

to be expensive

Conjugation

비싸다

bi-ssa-da

Present	*Past*	*Future / Guessing*	*Present Progressive*
비싸요	비쌌어요	비쌀 거예요	–
bissayo	bissasseoyo	bissal geoyeyo	

Imperative

–	–	–	–

Modifier

비싼	–	비쌀	비싸던	비쌌던
bissan		bissal	bissadeon	bissattteon

Want	*Can*
–	비쌀 수 있어요
	bissal su isseoyo

Don't (Imperative)	*Whether or not*		
–	비싼지	비쌌는지	비쌀지
	bissanji	bissanneunji	bissaljji

(tell someone) that	*(tell someone) to*
비싸다고	–
bissadago	

73

Sample Sentences

1. 왜 이렇게 비싸요?
   Why is it so expensive?

2. 영국은 물가가 비싸다고 들었어요.
   I heard that prices are expensive in the U.K.

3. 비싼 물건이라고 다 좋은 건 아니에요.
   Just because it's expensive doesn't mean that it's good.

4. 수공예 제품이라 비쌀 수 있어요.
   Since it's handmade, it can be expensive.

5. 수입한 물건이라 비쌀 거예요.
   Since it's an imported item, it is going to be expensive.

Quiz

1. 유키에 씨가 일본은 물가가 (   ) 했어요.
   Yukie said prices are expensive in Japan.

2. 유명한 디자이너가 디자인한 거라 (   ).
   Since a famous designer designed it, it can be expensive.

3. 한정판이라 (   ).
   Since it's a limited-edition, it is going to be expensive.

Answers :
1. 비싸다고 / 2. 비쌀 수 있어요 / 3. 비쌀 거예요

제 사진 찍지 마세요.

Don't take my pictures, please.

찍다

to take (a photo)

Conjugation

Present	Past	Future / Guessing	Present Progressive
찍어요	찍었어요	찍을 거예요	찍고 있어요
jjigeoyo	jjigeosseoyo	jjigeul geoyeyo	jjikkko isseoyo

Imperative

찍으세요	찍어요	찍어	찍어라
jjigeuseyo	jjigeoyo	jjigeo	jjigeora

Modifier

찍은	찍는	찍을	찍던	찍었던
jjigeun	jjingneun	jjigeul	jjik-tteon	jjigeottteon

Want	Can
찍고 싶어요	찍을 수 있어요
jjikkko sipeoyo	jjigeul su isseoyo

Don't (Imperative)		Whether or not		
찍지 마세요	찍는지	찍었는지	찍을지	
jjikjji maseyo	jjingneunji	jjigeonneunji	jjigeuljji	

(tell someone) that	(tell someone) to
찍는다고	찍으라고
jjingneundago	jjigeurago

Sample Sentences

1. 새 카메라 사면 사진 많이 찍을 거예요.
   If I buy a new camera, I will take a lot of pictures.

2. 저도 비싼 카메라 있으면 사진 잘 찍을 수 있어요.
   If I had an expensive camera, I could take good pictures.

3. 제 사진 찍지 마세요.
   Don't take my pictures, please.

4. 제가 찍은 사진 어때요?
   How is the photo I took?

5. 같이 사진 찍어요.
   Let's take a photo together.

Quiz

1. 이번에 여행 가면 사진 많이 (　　　　　).
   While I am on my trip this time, I will take a lot of pictures.

2. 박물관 안에서 사진 (　　　　　).
   Don't take any pictures inside the museum, please.

3. 내일 웃긴 사진 (　　　　).
   Let's take funny photos tomorrow.

Answers :

1. 찍을 거예요 / 2. 찍지 마세요 / 3. 찍어요

The Korean Verbs Guide - vol.2

졸다
to doze off

Conjugation

Present	Past	Future / Guessing	Present Progressive
졸아요	졸았어요	졸 거예요	졸고 있어요
jorayo	jorasseoyo	jol geoyeyo	jolgo isseoyo

Imperative

조세요	졸아요	졸아	졸아라
joseyo	jorayo	jora	jorara

Modifier

존	조는	졸	졸던	졸았던
jon	joneun	jol	joldeon	jorattteon

Want / Can

Want	Can
졸고 싶어요	졸 수 있어요
jolgo sipeoyo	jol su isseyo

Don't (Imperative) / Whether or not

Don't (Imperative)	Whether or not		
졸지 마세요	조는지	졸았는지	졸지
jolji maseyo	joneunji	joranneunji	joljji

(tell someone) that / (tell someone) to

(tell someone) that	(tell someone) to
존다고	–
jondago	

Sample Sentences

1. 오늘 시험 보다가 졸았어요.
   I dozed off while taking my exam today.

2. 운전 중에는 절대로 졸지 마세요.
   Please never doze off while you are driving.

3. 왜 자꾸 졸아요?
   Why do you keep dozing off?

4. 저도 그 영화 보면서 졸았던 기억이 있어요.
   I also remember dozing off while watching that movie.

5. 지금 교실 안에 조는 사람이 8명이나 돼요.
   There are about eight people dozing off in the classroom right now.

Quiz

1. 아까 밥 먹다가 (   ).
   I dozed off while I was eating earlier today.

2. 걸을 때는 (   ).
   Please don't doze off while you are walking.

3. 사무실 안에 (   ) 사람이 한 명도 없어요.
   There is no one dozing off in the office.

Answers :
1. 졸았어요 / 2. 졸지 마세요 / 3. 조는

쉬다
to rest
to take time off

Conjugation

쉬다
swi-da

Present	Past	Future / Guessing	Present Progressive
쉬어요	쉬었어요	쉴 거예요	쉬고 있어요
swieoyo	swieosseoyo	swil geoyeyo	swigo isseoyo

Imperative

쉬세요	쉬어요	쉬어	쉬어라
swiseyo	swieoyo	swieo	swieora

Modifier

쉰	쉬는	쉴	쉬던	쉬었던
swin	swineun	swil	swideon	swieottteon

Want	Can
쉬고 싶어요	쉴 수 있어요
swigo sipeoyo	swil su isseoyo

Don't (Imperative)	Whether or not		
쉬지 마세요	쉬는지	쉬었는지	쉴지
swiji maseyo	swineunji	swieonneunji	swiljji

(tell someone) that	(tell someone) to
쉰다고	쉬라고
swindago	swirago

Sample Sentences

1. 푹 쉬었어요?
   Have you rested up?

2. 쉬는 날이 언제예요?
   When is your day off?

3. 지금은 일 안 하고 쉬고 있어요.
   I am taking time off and not working now.

4. 주말에는 쉬고 싶어요.
   I want to rest on the weekend.

5. 이거 다 하면 쉴 수 있어요.
   If I finish this, I can rest.

The Korean Verbs Guide - vol.2

Quiz

1. 주연 씨, 어제 (   )?
   Jooyeon, did you have a day off yesterday?

2. (   ) 시간에 잠깐 밖에 나갈까요?
   Shall we go out for a minute during the break?

3. 오늘 시험 끝나서 내일부터 (   ).
   The exams ended today, so I can rest starting tomorrow.

Answers :
1. 쉬었어요 / 2. 쉬는 / 3. 쉴 수 있어요

84

크다
to be big,
to be large

Conjugation

크다
keu-da

Present	Past	Future / Guessing	Present Progressive
커요	컸어요	클 거예요	–
keoyo	keosseoyo	keul geoyeyo	

Imperative

–	–	–	–

Modifier

큰	–	클	크던	컸던
keun		keul	keudeon	keottteon

Want	Can
–	클 수 있어요
	keul su isseyo

Don't (Imperative)	Whether or not		
–	큰지	컸는지	클지
	keunji	keonneunji	keuljji

(tell someone) that	(tell someone) to
크다고	–
keudago	

The Korean Verbs Guide - vol.2

Sample Sentences

1. 얼마나 컸는지 기억나요?
   Do you remember how big it was?

2. 농구공보다 커요.
   It is bigger than a basketball.

3. 그 가방보다 클 거예요.
   It will be bigger than that bag.

4. 얼마나 큰지 알아요?
   Do you know how big it is?

5. 크다고 들었는데 별로 안 컸어요.
   I heard it was big, but it wasn't that big.

Quiz

1. 수박보다 훨씬 (   ).
   It's a lot bigger than a watermelon.

2. 저 산보다는 안 (   ).
   It won't be bigger than that mountain.

3. 그게 얼마나 (   ) 아는 사람 있어요?
   Is there anyone who knows how big it is?

Answers :
1. 커요 / 2. 클 거예요 / 3. 큰지

87

과자가 너무 작아서 다 먹고
나서도 배가 고팠어요.

Since the cookies were too small, even after I ate them all,
I still felt hungry.

작다

to be small

Conjugation

작다
jak-tta

Present	Past	Future / Guessing	Present Progressive
작아요	작았어요	작을 거예요	–
jagayo	jagasseoyo	jageul geoyeyo	

Imperative

–	–	–	–

Modifier

작은	–	작을	작던	작았던
jageun		jageul	jaktteon	jagattteon

Want	Can
–	작을 수 있어요
	jageul su isseoyo

Don't (Imperative)	Whether or not		
–	작은지	작았는지	작을지
	jageunji	jaganneunji	jageuljji

(tell someone) that	(tell someone) to
작다고	–
jakttago	

Sample Sentences

Track
76

1. 이 신발은 저한테는 좀 작아요.
   These shoes are a little small for me.

2. 거기 그 작은 방은 제 동생 방이에요.
   That small room over there is my little brother's room.

3. 작년에 작았던 옷이 살을 뺐더니 이제는 잘 맞아요.
   The clothes that were small on me last year now fit me well because I lost weight.

4. 치마가 작은지 안 작은지 볼 수 있게 입어 보세요.
   Please try this skirt on so that I can see if it's small or not (for you).

5. 이 바지는 제가 입어 봤을 때는 좀 작았어요.
   When I tried these pants on, they were a little small.

Quiz

1. 그 자켓은 제가 입기에는 좀 (   ).
   That jacket is a little small for me to wear.

2. 여기 (   ) 방은 누구 방이에요?
   Whose room is this small room?

3. 모자가 (   ) 안 (   ) 써 보기 전에는 몰라요.
   You don't know if a hat is small or not until you wear it.

Answers :
1. 작아요 / 2. 작은 / 3. 작은지, 작은지

91

졸리다

to be sleepy, to feel
sleepy; to be so boring
that it makes one sleepy

Conjugation

졸리다
jol·li·da

Present	Past	Future / Guessing	Present Progressive
졸려요	졸렸어요	졸릴 거예요	–
jollyeoyo	jollyeosseoyo	jollil geoyeyo	

Imperative

–	–	–	–

Modifier

졸린	–	졸릴	졸리던	졸렸던
jollin		jollil	jollideon	jollyeottteon

Want	Can
–	졸릴 수 있어요
	jollil su isseoyo

Don't (Imperative)	Whether or not		
–	졸린지	졸렸는지	졸릴지
	jollinji	jollyeonneunji	jolliljji

(tell someone) that	(tell someone) to
졸리다고	–
jollidago	

Sample Sentences

1. 어제 강의 정말 졸렸어요.
   Yesterday's lecture was really boring (and made me sleepy).

2. 밥 먹고 나면 누구나 졸려요.
   Everyone feels sleepy after they have a meal.

3. 어젯밤에 뭐 했길래 그렇게 졸린 눈을 하고 있어요?
   What did you do last night that made your eyes look so sleepy?

4. 영화 보러 간 친구가 졸리다고 문자를 보냈어요.
   My friend, who went to see a movie, texted me and said he's sleepy.

5. 아까 졸렸는데 지금은 괜찮아요.
   I was sleepy before, but I'm okay now.

Quiz

1. 오늘 회의 정말 (   ).
   Today's meeting was really boring (and made me sleepy).

2. 저는 밥 먹고 나면 항상 (   ).
   I always feel sleepy after I have a meal.

3. 어제는 하루종일 (   ) 어젯밤에 10시간 잤더니 오늘은 괜찮아요.
   I was sleepy all day long yesterday, but after sleeping for ten hours last night, I'm okay now.

Answers :
1. 졸렸어요 / 2. 졸려요 / 3. 졸렸는데

94

피하다

to avoid, to dodge; to duck (down)

Conjugation

피하다
pi-ha-da

Present	Past	Future / Guessing	Present Progressive
피해요	피했어요	피할 거예요	피하고 있어요
pihaeyo	pihaesseoyo	pihal geoyeyo	pihago isseoyo

Imperative

피하세요	피해요	피해	피해라
pihaseyo	pihaeyo	pihae	pihaera

Modifier

피한	피하는	피할	피하던	피했던
pihan	pihaneun	pihal	pihadeon	pihaettteon

Want	Can
피하고 싶어요	피할 수 있어요
pihago sipeoyo	pihal su isseoyo

Don't (Imperative)	Whether or not		
피하지 마세요	피하는지	피했는지	피할지
pihaji maseyo	pihaneunji	pihaenneunji	pihaljji

(tell someone) that	(tell someone) to
피한다고	피하라고
pihandago	piharago

The Korean Verbs Guide - vol.2

Sample Sentences

1. 저 피하는 이유가 뭐예요?
   What's the reason you are avoiding me?

2. 될 수 있으면 그런 상황은 피하고 싶어요.
   I want to avoid that kind of situation as much as I can.

3. 살 빼고 싶으면 패스트 푸드는 피하세요.
   If you want to lose weight, please avoid junk food.

4. 그 사람 만나는 게 조금 불편해서 일부러 피했어요.
   I felt uncomfortable meeting him, so I avoided him.

5. 꼭 하고 싶은 말이 있으니까 오늘은 저를 피하지 마세요.
   I have something I really want to tell you, so please don't avoid me.

Quiz

1. 유리 씨를 (   ) 이유를 말해 주세요.
   Please tell me the reason why you are avoiding Yuri.

2. 오늘 밤에 악몽 꾸고 싶지 않으면 공포 영화는 (   ).
   If you don't want to have a nightmare tonight, please avoid a horror
   movie.

3. 전해주고 싶은 게 있으니까 이따가 저 (   ).
   I have something I want to give you, so please don't avoid me later.

Answers :
1. 피하는 / 2. 피하세요 / 3. 피하지 마세요

화내다

to get angry;
to yell (at someone
out of anger)

Conjugation

Present	Past	Future / Guessing	Present Progressive
화내요	화냈어요	화낼 거예요	화내고 있어요
hwanaeyo	hwanaesseoyo	hwanael geoyeyo	hwanaego isseoyo

Imperative

화내세요	화내요	화내	화내라
hwanaeseyo	hwanaeyo	hwanae	hwanaera

Modifier

화낸	화내는	화낼	화내던	화냈던
hwanaen	hwanaeneun	hwanael	hwanaedeon	hwanaettteon

Want

화내고 싶어요
hwanaego sipeoyo

Can

화낼 수 있어요
hwanael su isseoyo

Don't (Imperative)

화내지 마세요
hwanaeji maseyo

Whether or not

화내는지	화냈는지	화낼지
hwanaeneunji	hwanaennuenji	hwanaeljji

(tell someone) that

화낸다고
hwanaendago

(tell someone) to

화내라고
hwanaerago

Sample Sentences

1. 제가 그런 거 아니니까 저한테 화내지 마세요.
   I didn't do it, so please don't be mad at me.

2. 그런 상황에서는 누구나 화낼 수 있어요.
   In that kind of situation, anyone can get angry.

3. 너무 화가 나서 저도 모르게 동생한테 화냈어요.
   I was so angry that I yelled at my little brother unintentionally.

4. 성민 씨가 우리한테 화낸 이유를 이제 알았어요.
   Now I know why Seongmin yelled at us.

5. 저는 민규 씨한테 화낸 기억이 없어요.
   I don't remember yelling at Min-gyu.

Quiz

1. 저하고는 관계 없는 일이니까 저한테 (   ).
   It has nothing to do with me, so please don't be mad at me.

2. 어제는 동생 때문에 화가 나서 동생한테 (   ).
   I was angry because of my little sister, so I yelled at her.

3. 지숙 씨가 (   ) 이유 알아요?
   Do you know why Jisook yelled at us?

Answers :
1. 화내지 마세요 / 2. 화냈어요 / 3. 화낸

The Korean Verbs Guide - vol.2

아프다

to be sick, to feel sick;
to hurt

Conjugation

아프다
a-peu-da

	Present	Past	Future / Guessing	Present Progressive
	아파요	아팠어요	아플 거예요	–
	apayo	apasseoyo	apeul geoyeyo	

Imperative

–	–	–	–

Modifier

아픈	–	아플	아프던	아팠던
apeun		apeul	apeudeon	apattteon

	Want		Can
	–		아플 수 있어요
			apeul su isseoyo

Don't (Imperative)		Whether or not		
아프지 마세요		아픈지	아팠는지	아플지
apeuji maseyo		apeunji	apanneunji	apeuljji

(tell someone) that		(tell someone) to
아프다고		–
apeudago		

Sample Sentences

1. 동생이 어디가 아픈지 물어 봐.
   Ask your little brother where it hurts.

2. 조금 아플 거예요.
   It will hurt a little.

3. 정말 아팠어요.
   It really hurt.

4. 아픈 사람은 방에 가서 쉬어요.
   People who are sick, go to the room and get some rest.

5. 아프다고 말을 안 해서 아픈지 몰랐어요.
   Since you didn't tell me you were sick, I didn't know you were sick.

Quiz

1. 별로 안 (   ).
   It won't hurt that much.

2. 별로 안 (   ).
   It didn't hurt much.

3. (   ) 사람은 병원에 가세요.
   People who are sick, please make sure to go see a doctor.

오토바이는 위험하니까
타지 마세요.

Motorcycles are dangerous so don't ride them.

타다
(transportation) to take, to ride, to get on

Conjugation

타다
ta-da

Present	Past	Future / Guessing	Present Progressive
타요	탔어요	탈 거예요	타고 있어요
tayo	tasseoyo	tal geoyeyo	tago isseoyo

Imperative

타세요	타요	타	타라
taseyo	tayo	ta	tara

Modifier

탄	타는	탈	타던	탔던
tan	taneun	tal	tadeon	tattteon

Want / Can

Want	Can
타고 싶어요	탈 수 있어요
tago sipeoyo	tal su isseoyo

Don't (Imperative) / Whether or not

Don't (Imperative)	Whether or not		
타지 마세요	타는지	탔는지	탈지
taji maseyo	taneunji	tanneunji	taljji

(tell someone) that / (tell someone) to

(tell someone) that	(tell someone) to
탄다고	타라고
tandago	tarago

Sample Sentences

1. 내일 제가 탈 기차는 KTX보다 느려요.
   The train I will be riding tomorrow is slower than the KTX.

2. 제가 어제 탔던 자전거는 지용 씨 거예요.
   The bicycle I rode yesterday was Jiyong's.

3. 오토바이는 위험하니까 타지 마세요.
   Motorcycles are dangerous, so don't ride them.

4. 지하철 말고 버스 탈 거예요.
   I'm going to take the bus, not the subway.

5. 제가 탄 버스가 갑자기 멈췄어요.
   The bus I'm riding in, suddenly stopped.

Quiz

1. 제가 다음 달에 (   ) 비행기는 다른 비행기들보다 커요.
   The airplane I'll be riding next month is bigger than other planes.

2. 위험하니까 혼자서는 (   ).
   It's dangerous, so don't ride it alone.

3. 우리 지난 주에 (   ) 자동차 이름이 뭐예요?
   What is the name of the car we rode last week?

Answers :
1. 탈 / 2. 타지 마세요 / 3. 탄 or 탔던

107

느끼다

to feel

The Korean Verbs Guide - vol.2

Conjugation

Present	Past	Future / Guessing	Present Progressive
느껴요	느꼈어요	느낄 거예요	느끼고 있어요
neukkyeoyo	neukkyeosseoyo	neukkil geoyeyo	neukkigo isseoyo

Imperative

느끼세요	느껴요	느껴	느껴라
neukkiseyo	neukkyeyo	neukkyeo	neukkyeora

Modifier

느낀	느끼는	느낄	느끼던	느꼈던
neukkin	neukkineun	neukkil	neukkideon	neukkyeottteon

Want	Can
느끼고 싶어요	느낄 수 있어요
neukkigo sipeoyo	neukkil su isseoyo

Don't (Imperative)	Whether or not		
느끼지 마세요	느끼는지	느꼈는지	느낄지
neukkiji maseyo	neukkineunji	neukkyeonneunji	neukkiljji

(tell someone) that	(tell someone) to
느낀다고	느끼라고
neukkindago	neukkirago

Sample Sentences

1. 이 영화를 보고 뭘 느꼈어요?
   What did you feel after you saw the movie?

2. 제가 느낀 감정을 솔직하게 이야기 할게요.
   I'll tell you how I honestly felt (about it).

3. 출근 안 하고 여행 가고 싶은 충동을 자주 느껴요.
   I often feel the urge not to go to work, but rather go on a trip.

4. 저도 그런 따뜻한 감정을 느끼고 싶어요.
   I want to feel that kind of warm feeling, too.

5. 오늘 그 두 사람 사이가 어색하다고 느낀 사람 저 말고 또 있어요?
   Is there anyone else who felt like it was awkward between those two people?

Quiz

1. 그 책을 읽고 뭘 (   )?
   How did you feel after you read that book?

2. 학교 안 가고 집에서 쉬고 싶은 충동을 자주 (   ).
   I often feel the urge not to go to school but to just rest at home.

3. 그 두 사람 사이에 뭔가 있다고 (   ) 사람?
   Who felt like there was something between those two people?

Answers :
1. 느꼈어요 / 2. 느껴요 / 3. 느낀

The Korean Verbs Guide - vol.2

죽다
to die

Conjugation

죽다
juk-tta

Present	Past	Future / Guessing	Present Progressive
죽어요	죽었어요	죽을 거예요	죽고 있어요
jugeoyo	jugeosseoyo	jugeul geoyeyo	jukkko isseoyo

Imperative

죽으세요	죽어요	죽어	죽어라
jugeuseyo	jugeoyo	jugeo	jugeora

Modifier

죽은	죽는	죽을	죽던	죽었던
jugeun	jungneun	jugeul	juktteon	jugeottteon

Want	Can
죽고 싶어요	죽을 수 있어요
jukkko sipeoyo	jugeul su isseoyo

Don't (Imperative)	Whether or not		
죽지 마세요	죽는지	죽었는지	죽을지
jukjji maseyo	jungneunji	jugeonneunji	jugeuljji

(tell someone) that	(tell someone) to
죽는다고	죽으라고
jungneundago	jugeurago

Sample Sentences

1. 저는 이 영화에서 누가 죽는지 알고 있어요.
   I know who dies in this film.

2. 저는 사람이 죽는 게임은 싫어해요.
   I don't like games where people die (in the game).

3. 죽은 사람이 자꾸 꿈에 나타난다고요?
   Are you saying a dead person keeps appearing in your dream?

4. 제가 어릴 때 기르던 고양이는 제가 15살 때 죽었어요.
   The cat I had when I was little died when I was 15.

5. 물을 안 주면 꽃이 금방 죽을 거예요.
   If you don't water the flower, it will die soon

Quiz

1. 이 소설에서 누가 (   ) 알아요?
   Do you know who dies in this novel?

2. 저희 집 강아지가 최근에 (   ).
   My dog died recently.

3. 먹이를 안 주면 금붕어가 (   ).
   If you don't feed the gold fish, they will die.

Answers :
1. 죽는지 / 2. 죽었어요 / 3. 죽을 거예요

113

느리다

to be slow

Conjugation

Present	Past	Future / Guessing	Present Progressive
느려요	느렸어요	느릴 거예요	–
neuryeoyo	neuryeosseoyo	neuril geoyeyo	

Imperative

–	–	–	–

Modifier

느린	–	느릴	느리던	느렸던
neurin		neuril	neurideon	neuryeotteon

Want

–

Can

느릴 수 있어요
neuril su isseoyo

Don't (Imperative)

–

Whether or not

느린지	느렸는지	느릴지
neurinji	neuryeonneunji	neuriljji

(tell someone) that

느리다고
neuridago

(tell someone) to

–

Sample Sentences

1. 느린 컴퓨터로 일하려니 효율이 떨어져요.
   I'm trying to work with a slow computer and it's really ineffective.

2. 얼마나 느린지 상상이 안 돼요.
   I can't imagine how slow it is.

3. 컴퓨터를 새로 사니까 제 옛날 컴퓨터가 얼마나 느렸는지 이제 알겠어요.
   Now that I've bought a new computer, I realize how slow my old computer was.

4. 여기는 인터넷 속도가 조금 느려요.
   The internet is a bit slow here.

5. 제 기억에는 정말 느렸어요.
   As far as I remember, it was very slow.

Quiz

1. (   ) 컴퓨터로 게임을 하려니 재미가 없어요.
   I'm trying to play a game on a slow computer and it's not really fun.

2. 얼마나 (   ) 알아요?
   Do you know how slow it is?

3. 저희 집은 인터넷 속도가 별로 안 (   ).
   The internet is not that slow in my house.

Answers :
1. 느린 / 2. 느린지 / 3. 느려요

같은 색깔의 버스가 많아요.

There are many buses with the same color.

같다

to be the same

Conjugation

같다
gat-tta

Present	*Past*	*Future / Guessing*	*Present Progressive*
같아요	같았어요	같을 거예요	–
gatayo	gatasseoyo	gateul geoyeyo	

Imperative

–	–	–	–

Modifier

같은	–	같을	같던	같았던
gateun		gateul	gattteon	gatattteon

Want	*Can*
–	같을 수 있어요
	gateul su isseoyo

Don't (Imperative)	*Whether or not*		
–	같은지	같았는지	같을지
	gateunji	gatanneunji	gateuljji

(tell someone) that	*(tell someone) to*
같다고	–
gatttago	

Sample Sentences

1. 가격이 같은지 물어봐 주세요.
Please ask if the price is the same.

2. 내일 같은 시간, 같은 장소에서 봐요.
I will see you tomorrow at the same place, same time.

3. 저랑 나이가 같다고요?
You said we are the same age?

4. 저랑 지은 씨는 몸무게는 다른데 키는 같아요.
Jieun and I have different weights, but our height is the same.

5. 같았는지 달랐는지 기억이 안 나요.
I don't remember if it was the same or if it was different.

Quiz

1. 시간도 ( ) 알려주세요.
Please let me know if the time is the same, too.

2. 다음 주에도 ( ) 시간에 볼까요?
Should we meet up at the same time next week, too?

3. ( ) 달랐는지 말해 주세요.
Please tell me if it was the same or if it was different.

Answers :
1. 같은지 / 2. 같은 / 3. 같았는지

나가다

to go out,
to get out

Conjugation

나가다
na-ga-da

Present	Past	Future / Guessing	Present Progressive
나가요	나갔어요	나갈 거예요	나가고 있어요
nagayo	nagasseoyo	nagal geoyeyo	nagago isseoyo

Imperative

나가세요	나가요	나가	나가라
nagaseyo	nagayo	naga	nagara

Modifier

나간	나가는	나갈	나가던	나갔던
nagan	naganeun	nagal	nagadeon	nagattteon

Want

		Can	
나가고 싶어요		나갈 수 있어요	
nagago sipeoyo		nagal su isseoyo	

Don't (Imperative)

Whether or not

나가지 마세요	나가는지	나갔는지	나갈지
nagaji maseyo	naganeunji	naganneunji	nagaljji

(tell someone) that

(tell someone) to

나간다고		나가라고	
nagandago		nagarago	

Sample Sentences

1. 저도 이제 나갈 거예요.
   I'm going to leave now, too.

2. 여기서 나가고 싶어요.
   I want to get out of here.

3. 정수 씨가 언제 나갔는지 알아요?
   Do you know when Jeong-su left?

4. 방금 나간 사람 누구예요?
   Who is the person who just left?

5. 윤지 씨가 벌써 나갔는지 몰랐어요.
   I didn't know Yoonji already left.

Quiz

1. 빨리 (   ).
   I want to get out of here quickly.

2. 아까 (   ) 사람 누군지 알아요?
   Do you know the person who left earlier?

3. 진수 씨가 언제 (   ) 알아요?
   Do you know when Jinsoo left?

123

울다
to cry, to sob

Conjugation

울다
ul-da

Present	Past	Future / Guessing	Present Progressive
울어요	울었어요	울 거예요	울고 있어요
ureoyo	ureosseoyo	ul geoyeyo	ulgo isseoyo

Imperative

우세요	울어요	울어	울어라
useyo	ureoyo	ureo	ureora

Modifier

운	우는	울	울던	울었던
un	uneun	ul	uldeon	ureottteon

Want

울고 싶어요
ulgo sipeoyo

Can

울 수 있어요
ul su isseoyo

Don't (Imperative)

울지 마세요
ulji maseyo

Whether or not

우는지	울었는지	울지
uneunji	ureonneunji	uljji

(tell someone) that

운다고
undago

(tell someone) to

울라고
ullago

Sample Sentences

1. 밤마다 옆집 아기가 울어요.
   The baby next door cries every night.

2. 슬프면 참지 말고 그냥 울어.
   If you are sad, don't hold back and just cry.

3. 그 영화 보고 안 울었어요?
   You didn't cry after watching that movie?

4. 제가 어떤 말을 해도 울지 마세요.
   Please don't cry no matter what I say.

5. 일이 잘 안 돼서 울고 싶어요.
   Things didn't go well, so I want to cry.

Quiz

1. 지민 씨는 그 책을 읽고 안 (   ).
   Jimin didn't cry after she read the book.

2. 무슨 일이 있어도 (   ).
   No matter what happens, please don't cry.

3. 엄마한테 혼나서 (   ).
   I was scolded by my mom, so I want to cry.

Answers :
1. 울었어요 / 2. 울지 마세요 / 3. 울고 싶어요

The Korean Verbs Guide - vol.2

누르다

to press;
to hit (a button)

Conjugation

누르다

nu-reu-da

Present	Past	Future / Guessing	Present Progressive
눌러요	눌렀어요	누를 거예요	누르고 있어요
nulleoyo	nulleosseoyo	nureul geoyeyo	nureugo isseoyo

Imperative

누르세요	눌러요	눌러	눌러라
nureuseyo	nulleoyo	nulleo	nulleora

Modifier

누른	누르는	누를	누르던	눌렀던
nureun	nureuneun	nureul	nureudeon	nulleottteon

Want / *Can*

Want	Can
누르고 싶어요	누를 수 있어요
nureugo sipeoyo	nureul su isseoyo

Don't (Imperative) / *Whether or not*

Don't (Imperative)	Whether or not		
누르지 마세요	누르는지	눌렀는지	누를지
nureuji maseyo	nureuneunji	nulleonneunji	nureuljji

(tell someone) that / *(tell someone) to*

(tell someone) that	(tell someone) to
누른다고	누르라고
nureundago	nureurago

Sample Sentences

1. 더 세게 눌러요.
   Please push it hard.

2. 언니가 이럴 때는 F5키를 누르라고 했어요.
   My older sister told me to press the F5 button when that happens.

3. 아프니까 너무 세게 누르지 마세요.
   It hurts, so please don't press on it too hard.

4. 이 단추 누가 눌렀는지 알아요?
   Do you know who pushed this button?

5. 주문을 하실 때는 이 버튼을 누르세요.
   When you order, please push this button.

Quiz

1. 엄마가 밥을 하려면 이 버튼을 (   ) 하셨어요.
   My mom told me to press this button to cook the rice.

2. 엔터키 누가 (   ) 말해 주세요.
   Please tell me who pressed(hit) the enter button.

3. 필요한 게 있으면 이 버튼을 (   ).
   If you need anything, please push this button.

밀다
to push

The Korean Verbs Guide - vol.2

Conjugation

밀다
mil-da

Present	Past	Future / Guessing	Present Progressive
밀어요	밀었어요	밀 거예요	밀고 있어요
mireoyo	mireosseoyo	mil geoyeyo	milgo isseoyo

Imperative

미세요	밀어요	밀어	밀어라
miseyo	mireoyo	mireo	mireora

Modifier

민	미는	밀	밀던	밀었던
min	mineun	mil	mildeon	mireottteon

Want

밀고 싶어요
milgo sipeoyo

Can

밀 수 있어요
mil su isseoyo

Don't (Imperative)

밀지 마세요
milji maseyo

Whether or not

미는지	밀었는지	밀지
mineunji	mireonneunji	miljji

(tell someone) that

민다고
mindago

(tell someone) to

밀라고
millago

Sample Sentences

1. 제 등을 누가 밀었는지 아세요?
   Do you know who pushed me in the back?

2. 누가 뒤에서 자꾸 밀어요.
   Someone keeps pushing me in the back.

3. 위험하니까 여기서 밀지 마세요.
   Don't push me here because it's dangerous.

4. 두 손으로 동시에 미세요.
   Please push it with both hands at the same time.

5. 제가 뒤에서 밀었어요.
   I pushed it from behind.

Quiz

1. 버스 정류장에서 누가 절 (   ) 아세요?
   Do you know who pushed me at the bus stop?

2. 승민 씨가 자꾸 (   ).
   Seung-min keeps pushing me.

3. 제가 신호를 보내면 (   ).
   Push it when I give you the sign.

Answers :
1. 밀었는지 / 2. 밀어요 / 3. 미세요 or 밀어요

The Korean Verbs Guide - vol.2

당기다

to pull

Conjugation

당기다
dang-gi-da

Present	Past	Future / Guessing	Present Progressive
당겨요	당겼어요	당길 거예요	당기고 있어요
dang-gyeoyo	dang-gyeosseoyo	dang-gil geoyeyo	dang-gigo isseoyo

Imperative

당기세요	당겨요	당겨	당겨라
dang-giseyo	dang-gyeoyo	dang-gyeo	dang-gyeora

Modifier

당긴	당기는	당길	당기던	당겼던
dang-gin	dang-gineun	dang-gil	dang-gideon	dang-gyeottteon

Want / Can

Want	Can
당기고 싶어요	당길 수 있어요
dang-gigo sipeoyo	dang-gil su isseoyo

Don't (Imperative)	Whether or not		
당기지 마세요	당기는지	당겼는지	당길지
dang-giji maseyo	dang-gineunji	dang-gyeonneunji	dang-giljji

(tell someone) that	(tell someone) to
당긴다고	당기라고
dang-gindago	dang-girago

The Korean Verbs Guide - vol.2

Sample Sentences

Track
90

1. 여기에는 이 줄을 당기라고 써 있어요.
   Here, it says to pull this cord.

2. 그쪽에서 당기세요.
   Please pull it from there.

3. 어디를 당기는지 아세요?
   Do you know where we should pull?

4. 밀지 말고 당기세요.
   Please don't push, but pull.

5. 더 세게 당길 수 있어요?
   Can you pull it harder?

Quiz

1. 줄을 (   ) 써 있어요?
   Does it say to pull the cord?

2. 지영 씨가 (   )요.
   Jiyoung, you pull it, please.

3. 혼자 (   )?
   Can you pull it by yourself?

그냥 아무 곳에나
놓으세요.

Just put it anywhere please.

놓다
to put, to place
(something)

Conjugation

Present	Past	Future / Guessing	Present Progressive
놓아요	놓았어요	놓을 거예요	놓고 있어요
noayo	noasseoyo	no-eul geoyeyo	noko isseoyo

Imperative

놓으세요	놓아요	놓아	놓아라
no-euseyo	noayo	noa	noara

Modifier

놓은	놓는	놓을	놓던	놓았던
no-eun	nonneun	noeul	noteon	noattteon

Want	Can
놓고 싶어요	놓을 수 있어요
noko sipeoyo	no-eul su isseoyo

Don't (Imperative)	Whether or not		
놓지 마세요	놓는지	놓았는지	놓을지
nochi maseyo	nonneunji	noanneunji	no-euljji

(tell someone) that	(tell someone) to
놓는다고	놓으라고
nonneundago	no-eurago

Sample Sentences

Track
91

1. 이 꽃병은 식탁 위에 놓고 싶어요.
   I want to put this flower vase on the dining table.

2. 화분을 어디에 놓을지 아직도 못 정했어요?
   Have you still not decided where you are going to put the flowerpot?

3. 그냥 아무 곳에나 놓으세요.
   Just put it anywhere, please.

4. 제가 가방을 여기에 놓을지 어떻게 알았어요?
   How did you know I would put my bag here?

5. 새로 산 침대는 어디에 놓을 거예요?
   Where are you going to put the new bed that you bought?

Quiz

1. 새로 산 의자는 책상 앞에 (   ).
   I want to put the new chair I bought in front of the desk.

2. 이 토끼 인형 어디에 (   ) 정했어요?
   Have you decided where to put this stuffed rabbit?

3. 제 옆에 (   ).
   Please put it next to me.

Answers :
1. 놓고 싶어요 / 2. 놓을지 / 3. 놓아주세요

끝나다

to be over;
something is finished

The Korean Verbs Guide - vol.2

Conjugation

끝나다
kkeun-na-da

Present	*Past*	*Future / Guessing*	*Present Progressive*
끝나요	끝났어요	끝날 거예요	–
kkeunnayo	kkeunnasseoyo	kkeunnal geoyeyo	

Imperative

–	–	–	–

Modifier

끝난	끝나는	끝날	끝나던	끝났던
kkeunnan	kkeunnaneun	kkeunnal	kkeunadeon	kkeunnattteon

Want	*Can*
–	끝날 수 있어요
	kkeunnal su isseoyo

Don't (Imperative)	*Whether or not*		
–	끝나는지	끝났는지	끝날지
	kkeunnaneunji	kkeunnanneunji	kkeunnaljji

(tell someone) that	*(tell someone) to*
끝난다고	–
kkeunnandago	

141

Sample Sentences

1. 언제 끝났어요?
   When did it finish?

2. 내일이면 끝난다고 했어요.
   They said it will be finished tomorrow.

3. 곧 방학이 끝날 거예요.
   The school vacation will be over soon.

4. 행사가 벌써 끝났는지 몰랐어요.
   I didn't know the event was already over.

5. 이 영화 몇 시에 끝나는지 아세요?
   Do you know what time the movie finishes?

Quiz

1. 다음 주에 (   ) 들었어요.
   I heard it will be finished next week.

2. 한 시간 후에 수업이 (   ).
   The class will be over in an hour.

3. 학교가 몇 시에 (   ) 물어보세요.
   Please ask her what time school finishes.

가르치다

to teach

Conjugation

ga-reu-chi-da

Present	*Past*	*Future / Guessing*	*Present Progressive*
가르쳐요	가르쳤어요	가르칠 거예요	가르치고 있어요
gareuchyeoyo	gareuchyeosseoyo	gareuchil geoyeyo	gareuchigo isseoyo

Imperative

가르치세요	가르쳐요	가르쳐	가르쳐라
gareuchiseyo	gareuchyeoyo	gareuchyeo	gareuchyeora

Modifier

가르친	가르치는	가르칠	가르치던	가르쳤던
gareuchin	gareuchineun	gareuchil	gareuchideon	gareuchyeottteon

Want / *Can*

Want	*Can*
가르치고 싶어요	가르칠 수 있어요
gareuchigo sipeoyo	gareuchil su isseoyo

Don't (Imperative) / *Whether or not*

Don't (Imperative)	*Whether or not*		
가르치지 마세요	가르치는지	가르쳤는지	가르칠지
gareuchiji maseyo	gareuchineunji	gareuchyeonneunji	gareuchiljji

(tell someone) that / *(tell someone) to*

(tell someone) that	*(tell someone) to*
가르친다고	가르치라고
gareuchindago	gareuchirago

Sample Sentences

1. 그런 건 아이들한테 가르치지 마세요.
   Please don't teach such things to the children.

2. 저는 고등학교에서 음악을 가르쳐요.
   I teach music at a high school.

3. 어디에서 가르친다고 했죠?
   Where did you say you teach at?

4. 이 반은 제니퍼 선생님이 영어를 가르칠 거예요.
   Teacher Jennifer will teach English in this class.

5. 어제 가르친 중국어 단어를 학생들이 벌써 다 잊어버렸어요.
   The students already forgot all the Chinese words I taught them yesterday.

Quiz

1. 희수 씨는 대학교에서 수학을 (   ).
   Heesu teaches math at a university.

2. 뭐 (   ) 했죠?
   What did you say you teach?

3. 지난 주에 (   ) 수학 공식을 기억하는 학생이 한 명도 없
   어요.
   There's no student who remembers the math formula I taught last
   week.

Answers :
1. 가르쳐요 / 2. 가르친다고 / 3. 가르친

145

내다

to hand in, to submit; to pay;
to publish; to suggest (idea);
to put up (an advertisement)

Conjugation

Present	Past	Future / Guessing	Present Progressive
내요	냈어요	낼 거예요	내고 있어요
naeyo	naesseoyo	nael geoyeyo	naego isseoyo

Imperative

내세요	내요	내	내라
naeseyo	naeyo	nae	naera

Modifier

낸	내는	낼	내던	냈던
naen	naeneun	nael	naedeon	naettteon

Want	Can
내고 싶어요	낼 수 있어요
naego sipeoyo	nael su isseoyo

Don't (Imperative)	Whether or not		
내지 마세요	내는지	냈는지	낼지
naeji maseyo	naeneunji	naenneunji	naeljji

(tell someone) that	(tell someone) to
낸다고	내라고
naendago	naerago

147

Sample Sentences

Track
94

1. 누가 돈 낼지 정했어요?
   Have you guys decided who's going to pay?

2. 제가 냈어요.
   I paid.

3. 신문에 광고를 어떻게 내는지 아세요?
   Do you know how to put up an ad in a newspaper?

4. 어제 회사에 사표를 냈어요.
   I submitted my resignation letter at work yesterday.

5. 핸드폰으로 세금 낼 수 있어요?
   Can we pay the tax with our cellphone?

Quiz

1. 지석 씨가 (   ).
   Jiseok paid.

2. 이번 커피 값은 누가 (   ) 정했어요?
   Have you guys decided who's going to pay for the coffee this time?

3. 인터넷으로 벌금 (   )?
   Can we pay the fine over the internet?

Answers :
1. 냈어요 / 2. 낼지 / 3. 낼 수 있어요

The Korean Verbs Guide - vol.2

빼다

to take out, to pull out

Conjugation

Present	Past	Future / Guessing	Present Progressive
빼요	뺐어요	뺄 거예요	빼고 있어요
ppaeyo	ppaesseoyo	ppael geoyeyo	ppaego isseoyo

Imperative

빼세요	빼요	빼	빼라
ppaeseyo	ppaeyo	ppae	ppaera

Modifier

뺀	빼는	뺄	빼던	뺐던
ppaen	ppaeneun	ppael	ppaedeon	ppaettteon

Want

빼고 싶어요	뺄 수 있어요
ppaego sipeoyo	ppael su isseoyo

Can

Don't (Imperative)

빼지 마세요	빼는지	뺐는지	뺄지
ppaeji maseyo	ppaeneunji	ppaenneunji	ppaeljji

Whether or not

(tell someone) that

뺀다고	빼라고
ppaendago	ppaerago

(tell someone) to

Sample Sentences

1. 주머니에서 손 빼세요.
   Please take your hands out of your pocket.

2. 왜 저를 팀에서 뺐어요?
   Why did you take me off of the team?

3. 못이 위험하니까 빼라고 말했는데 아직 그대로 있네요.
   I told them to pull this nail out because it is dangerous, but it is still here.

4. 저는 작년에 사랑니를 뺐어요.
   I got my wisdom teeth pulled last year.

5. 오늘 세미나에 안 온 사람들 이름을 명단에서 빼고 있어요.
   I'm taking off the names of the people who didn't come to the seminar today.

Quiz

1. 저를 그룹에서 (   ) 이유가 뭔가요?
   What is the reason that you took me out of the group?

2. 못을 (   ) 했는데 왜 안 (   )?
   I told you to pull this nail out, but why didn't you do it?

3. 어제 드디어 치과에서 사랑니 (   ).
   I finally got my wisdom teeth taken out yesterday at the dentist.

Answers :
1. 뺐어 / 2. 빼라고, 뺐어요 / 3. 뺐어요

151

넣다

to put in, to insert

Conjugation

넣다
neo-ta

Present	Past	Future / Guessing	Present Progressive
넣어요	넣었어요	넣을 거예요	넣고 있어요
neo-eoyo	neo-eosseoyo	neo-eul geoyeyo	neoko isseoyo

Imperative

넣으세요	넣어요	넣어	넣어라
neo-euseyo	neo-eoyo	neo-eo	neo-eora

Modifier

넣은	넣는	넣을	넣던	넣었던
neo-eun	neonneun	neo-eul	neoteon	neo-eotteon

Want

넣고 싶어요
neoko sipeoyo

Can

넣을 수 있어요
neo-eul su isseoyo

Don't (Imperative)

넣지 마세요
neochi maseyo

Whether or not

넣는지	넣었는지	넣을지
neonneunji	neo-eonneunji	neo-euljji

(tell someone) that

넣는다고
neonneundago

(tell someone) to

넣으라고
neo-eurago

Sample Sentences

1. 제 커피에는 설탕 넣지 마세요.
   Please do not put sugar in my coffee.

2. 제 가방에 뭐 넣었어요?
   What did you put in my bag?

3. 책은 가방에 넣으세요.
   Please put the book in the bag.

4. 여기에 100원짜리 동전만 넣으라고 써 있어요.
   It says to only put 100 won coins in here.

5. 아까 케이크에 넣은 우유가 상했었나 봐요.
   The milk that we put in the cake a little while ago seems to have been spoiled.

Quiz

1. 제 수프에 후추 (   ).
   Please don't put pepper in my soup.

2. 돈은 주머니에 (   ).
   Please put the money in your pocket.

3. 샌드위치에 (   ) 치즈가 맛있어요.
   The cheese we put in the sandwich is yummy

Answers :
1. 넣지 마세요 / 2. 넣으세요 or 넣어요 / 3. 넣은

요즘 재미있는 걸 배우고 있어요.

I'm learning something interesting these days.

배우다
to learn

The Korean Verbs Guide - vol.2

Conjugation

Present	Past	Future / Guessing	Present Progressive
배워요	배웠어요	배울 거예요	배우고 있어요
baewoyo	baewosseoyo	baeul geoyeyo	baeugo isseoyo

Imperative

배우세요	배워요	배워	배워라
baeuseyo	baewoyo	baewo	baewora

Modifier

배운	배우는	배울	배우던	배웠던
bae-un	bae-uneun	bae-ul	bae-udeon	baewottteon

Want	Can
배우고 싶어요	배울 수 있어요
bae-ugo sipeoyo	bae-ul su isseoyo

Don't (Imperative)	Whether or not		
배우지 마세요	배우는지	배웠는지	배울지
bae-uji maseyo	bae-uneunji	baewonneunji	bae-uljji

(tell someone) that	(tell someone) to
배운다고	배우라고
bae-undago	bae-urago

Sample Sentences

1. 우리 같이 요리 배워요.
   Let's learn how to cook together.

2. 저 사람한테는 배우지 마세요.
   Don't learn from that person.

3. 어디서 한국어 배울 수 있어요?
   Where can I learn Korean?

4. 올 여름에는 서핑을 배울 거예요.
   I'm going to learn how to surf this summer.

5. 지난주에 뭐 배웠는지 기억나요?
   Do you remember what we learned last week?

Quiz

1. 이번 여름에 같이 수영 (   ).
   Let's learn how to swim together this summer.

2. 내년 봄부터는 피아노 (   ).
   Starting from next spring, I'm going to learn how to play the piano.

3. 지난 금요일에 뭐 (   ) 말해 주세요.
   Please tell me what you learned last Friday.

Answers :
1. 배워요 / 2. 배울 거예요 / 3. 배웠는지

The Korean Verbs Guide - vol.2

되다

to become;
(something) is done

Conjugation

되다
doe-da

Present	Past	Future / Guessing	Present Progressive
돼요 dwaeyo	됐어요 dwaesseoyo	될 거예요 doel geoyeyo	되고 있어요 doego isseoyo

Imperative

되세요 doeseyo	돼요 dwaeyo	돼 dwae	돼라 dwaera

Modifier

된 doen	되는 doeneun	될 doel	되던 doedeon	됐던 dwaettteon

Want

되고 싶어요
doego sipeoyo

Can

될 수 있어요
doel su isseoyo

Don't (Imperative)

되지 마세요
doeji maseyo

Whether or not

되는지 doeneunji	됐는지 dwaenneunji	될지 doeljji

(tell someone) that

된다고
doendago

(tell someone) to

되라고
doerago

The Korean Verbs Guide - vol.2

Sample Sentences

1. 벌써 겨울이 됐어요.
   It has already become winter.

2. 피아니스트가 되는 것이 꿈이었어요.
   My dream was to become a pianist.

3. 누가 1등이 됐는지 너무 궁금해요.
   I curious to know who became number 1.

4. 조금만 기다리면 요리가 다 된다고 했어요.
   He said if you wait just a little, the food would be done.

5. 오늘 너무 더워서 얼음이 물이 됐어요.
   Today was so hot that the ice became water.

Quiz

1. 대회 연습을 하는 사이에 벌써 1월이 (   ).
   While we were practicing for the contest, it had already became January.

2. 저는 어렸을 때 비행기 조종사가 (   ) 것이 꿈이었어요.
   When I was little, my dream was to become a pilot.

3. 누가 대통령이 (   ) 알아요?
   Do you know who became the president?

Answers :
1. 됐어요 / 2. 되는 / 3. 됐는지

161

걸다
to hang

Conjugation

Present	*Past*	*Future / Guessing*	*Present Progressive*
걸어요	걸었어요	걸 거예요	걸고 있어요
georeoyo	georeosseoyo	geol geoyeyo	geolgo isseoyo
			걸려 있어요*
			geollyeo isseoyo

Imperative

거세요	걸어요	걸어	걸어라
geoseyo	georeoyo	georeo	georeora

Modifier

건	거는	걸	걸던	걸었던
geon	geoneun	geol	geoldeon	georeottteon

Want

걸고 싶어요
geolgo sipeoyo

Can

걸 수 있어요
geol su isseoyo

Don't (Imperative)

걸지 마세요
geolji maseyo

Whether or not

거는지	걸었는지	걸지
geoneunji	georeonneunji	geoljji

(tell someone) that

건다고
geondago

(tell someone) to

걸라고
geollago

*present status

Sample Sentences

1. 이 시계 어디에 걸 거예요?
   Where are you going to hang up this clock?

2. 건물 왼쪽에 간판을 걸라고 시켰어요.
   I ordered them to hang up a sign on the left side of the building.

3. 이 벽에는 아무것도 걸지 마세요.
   Don't hang up anything on this wall.

4. 옷걸이에 걸었던 옷이 조금 구겨졌어요.
   The clothes that I hung up on the hanger became wrinkled.

5. 망치하고 못만 있으면 이런 작은 시계는 벽에 금방 걸 수 있어요.
   If you have a hammer and a nail, you can hang up a small clock, like this one,
   quickly.

Quiz

1. 이 사진 도대체 언제 벽에 (   )?
   When on earth are you going to hang up this picture?

2. 엄마가 이걸 이쪽 벽에 (   ) 하셨어요.
   My mom told me to hang this up on the wall over here.

3. 저 옷걸이에는 아무 옷도 (   ).
   Don't hang up any clothes on that hanger.

예쁘다

to be pretty,
to be beautiful

Conjugation

예쁘다
ye-ppeu-da

Present	Past	Future / Guessing	Present Progressive
예뻐요 yeppeoyo	예뻤어요 yeppeosseoyo	예쁠 거예요 yeppeul geoyeyo	–

Imperative			
–	–	–	–

Modifier				
예쁜 yeppeun	–	예쁠 yeppeul	예쁘던 yeppeudeon	예뻤던 yeppeottteon

Want	Can
–	예쁠 수 있어요 yeppeul su isseoyo

Don't (Imperative)	Whether or not		
–	예쁜지 yeppeunji	예뻤는지 yeppeonneunji	예쁠지 yeppeuljji

(tell someone) that	(tell someone) to
예쁘다고 yeppeudago	–

The Korean Verbs Guide - vol.2

Sample Sentences

1. 반에서 제일 예뻤던 아이라고 기억해요.
   I remember her being the prettiest girl in our class.

2. 어떤 색이 예쁠지 모르겠어요.
   I don't know what color would look pretty.

3. 이 글씨체 너무 예뻐요.
   This writing style is so pretty.

4. 선물을 예쁜 포장지에 싸서 주고 싶어요.
   I want to wrap the present in pretty wrapping paper, then give it to her.

5. 이 가방 친구들이 예쁘다고 칭찬했어요.
   My friends complimented my bag, saying that it was pretty.

Quiz

1. 수현 씨가 쓰고 있는 모자 정말 (   ).
   The hat Soohyeon is wearing is really pretty.

2. 편지는 (   ) 봉투에 담으세요.
   Please put your letter in a pretty envelope.

3. 같은 반 친구가 제가 어제 새로 산 치마가 (   ) 했어요.
   My classmate told me that the skirt I bought yesterday is pretty.

Answers :
1. 예쁘네요 / 2. 예쁜 / 3. 예쁘다고

You can download the audio recordings for the words
and sample sentences used in this book at
https://talktomeinkorean.com/audio.